I0407080

MONEY MATTERS

Empowering the Youth with Financial Literacy

Joshua Paulus

"Nurture young minds with the art of financial wisdom, for in equipping our children with the knowledge of money's true value, we sow the seeds of a resilient and prosperous future."

PAULUS

CONTENTS

Title Page

Epigraph

Preface

Chapter 1 Earning and Saving Money   1

chapter 2 Budgeting and Spending Wisely   24

Chapter 3 Banking and Financial Institutions   49

Chapter 4 Planning for the Future   75

Chapter 5 Making Smart Financial Choices   109

Review and Recap   130

About The Author   135

PREFACE

This book has been crafted with one essential purpose: to empower young people like you with the knowledge and understanding of money topics and financial literacy. We believe that equipping you with these invaluable skills is one of the most crucial responsibilities we can undertake.

In today's rapidly evolving society, financial literacy plays an integral role in shaping a successful and secure future. Yet, it's unfortunate that financial education is not widely taught in schools. We recognize this gap and aim to bridge it by providing you with the tools to navigate the intricate world of finance confidently.

Throughout these pages, we will delve into essential money topics, from budgeting and saving strategies to understanding banking, investments, and entrepreneurship. By unraveling these concepts in a relatable and engaging manner, we hope to instill in you the confidence to make informed financial decisions and lay the groundwork for a prosperous life.

We firmly believe that financial literacy is not just a desirable skill but a necessary one. As you embark on this learning journey, we encourage you to embrace curiosity and a growth mindset. Remember that learning about money is not about becoming a financial expert overnight but rather about building a strong foundation for a lifetime of financial empowerment.

So, dear reader, we invite you to dive in, explore, and take charge of your financial destiny. Let this book be your guide to navigate the financial landscape and make well-informed choices that will shape your future. Together, let us embark on this empowering quest, for the knowledge you gain here will not only enrich your life but also benefit generations to come.

CHAPTER 1
EARNING AND
SAVING MONEY

"True wealth lies not in the accumulation of material possessions, but in the wisdom to understand and navigate the intricacies of money. Financial literacy is the key that unlocks the door to freedom, allowing us to live a life of tranquility and self-reliance."

1.1 Understanding the Value of Money

"Know that the true value of money lies not in its possession, but in the wisdom of how it is earned, saved, and shared."

Introducing The Concept Of Money And Its Importance In Our Lives

Welcome, young money enthusiasts! In this book, we embark on an exciting journey to explore the wonderful world of money and its value. Money plays a remarkable role in our lives, allowing us to obtain what we need and want. Learning about money early on empowers us to make intelligent financial decisions, build a secure future, and fulfill our dreams. However, what exactly is money, and why is it so important? Well, money is a medium of exchange that we use to buy goods and services. It comes in different forms, such as coins, paper bills, and digital currency. While it may seem like an ordinary piece of paper or shiny metal, money holds incredible power and potential. This chapter will unravel the secrets of money's value and why it matters. We will delve into earning, saving, and spending money wisely.

Along the way, we will encounter fascinating stories and practical examples to help us understand how money can shape our lives and the world around us. However, before we embark on this enlightening journey, let us reflect momentarily. Have you ever wondered why we need money? Why can't we get everything we want for free? Well, my curious friends, the truth is that resources in this world, while vast, are limited, while our wants and needs are boundless. Money is a fair and efficient system to exchange goods and services, allowing us to obtain what we desire by trading it for something of equal value. Think, I want a boat, but all I have is money. You have built a beautiful boat, but what you need is some money. So, we can trade my money for your boat, and we are both happy. This is capitalism, the system we live in in the United States. An even exchange for goods and services; I got what I wanted, and you got what you wanted, and we made a deal with as much knowledge and information as possible.

Understanding the value of money is not just about counting coins or bills; it is about recognizing the effort and hard work that goes into earning it. As we learn to appreciate the value of money, we develop essential life skills such as budgeting, saving, and making informed choices. These skills will enable us to prioritize our needs over wants, plan for the future, and accomplish our goals.

Throughout this chapter, we will embark on exciting adventures to grasp the actual value of money. So, get ready to unlock the secrets of financial independence, gain confidence in managing your finances, and discover money's immense potential. Remember, knowledge is the key to financial success, and together, we will unlock a world of opportunities! Are you excited? I know I am! Let's dive right in and embark on our marvelous journey to learn about the value of money.

1.2 Needs vs Wants

W ants A little story about wants vs. needs. Once upon a time, a young boy named Silas lived in a small town in the shadow of the Hoh Rainforest, nestled along the sea. Silas was an imaginative and curious child, always eager to explore the wonders of the world. He had a heart full of dreams and a mind filled with wild desires. Silas embarked on an adventure to his favorite farmers market one sunny morning. The market was bustling, brimming with delightful sights, smells, and sounds.

As he wandered through the stalls, his eyes twinkled with excitement at the array of toys, games, and treats on display. Silas discovered a dazzling, golden toy sword adorned with sparkling polished river stones in one beautifully decorated booth. Its enchanting allure captured his attention, and he felt an irresistible urge to possess it. He believed in his heart that this sword was what he truly wanted; what he felt would bring him immense joy and make him feel invincible.

In a flurry of anticipation, Silas approached

the merchant, holding his precious coins tightly. However, just as he was about to make his purchase, an older man with a short, scruffy white beard appeared beside him. The older man had a wise and gentle presence that radiated wisdom. "Ah, young one," the old man said kindly, "before you make your choice, allow me to share a tale of needs and wants." Intrigued, Silas paused, eager to listen and learn.

The older man began his tale. "In a distant kingdom, there was a young prince named Alexander. He was blessed with riches and surrounded by opulence. However, despite having everything he desired, Alexander felt deep emptiness. He realized that his wants had consumed him, leaving little room for true happiness." Silas listened intently, his eyes wide with wonder. The old man continued, "One day, Alexander encountered a wise sage who shared the secret to lasting fulfillment.

The sage spoke of distinguishing between needs and wants and the importance of finding contentment in simplicity." Silas pondered the lesson, his eyes shifting from the golden sword to the older man. Suddenly, the allure of the toy sword began to fade as he realized it was merely a want and not a genuine need. Silas thanked the older man with newfound clarity and returned the golden sword to its place. Instead, he used his coins to purchase a practical and sturdy pair of shoes, as his old ones had worn out.

Silas felt a sense of fulfillment and wisdom fill his heart as he walked away from the market. He understood that needs, such as comfortable shoes, were essential for his well-being, while wants, like the golden sword, were merely fleeting desires that would bring temporary pleasure. From that day forward, Silas carried the lesson of needs versus wants in his heart. He became a wise and discerning young boy, making thoughtful choices when spending his resources. He knew true happiness lay not in accumulating possessions but in appreciating and fulfilling his genuine needs.

Let Silas's story remind us that the understanding and balance between the two lead us to a life of true contentment and joy in the realm of needs and wants.

Differentiating Between Essential Needs And Wants

ESSENTIAL NEEDS are the fundamental requirements for our survival and well-being. They encompass the basic necessities that we cannot do without. These needs include:

Food: Nourishment is essential for our bodies to function properly. We need a balanced diet with energy and nutrients to stay healthy.

Clothing: Clothes protect us from the elements and help us maintain our dignity. They provide warmth, protection, cover our bodies and help demonstrate to the world our identity.

Shelter: Having a safe and comfortable place to live is essential. Shelter protects us from the elements and provides security, privacy, and a sense of belonging.

These three needs—food, clothing, and shelter—are vital for our physical and emotional well-being. They form the foundation of a fulfilling life and should be prioritized when managing our finances.

WANTS, on the other hand, go beyond our essential needs. They are desires or preferences that enhance our lives but are unnecessary for survival. Wants may include:
Toys and Games: Fun and entertainment are an important part of life, but toys and games fall into the wants category. They provide enjoyment and recreation but are not essential for our well-being.

Treats and Luxuries: Fancy treats, luxury items, and extravagant experiences may bring temporary pleasure, but they are not essential for our basic needs. These are things we can live without, even though they may be enjoyable to have occasionally.

Understanding the difference between "needs and

wants" helps us make informed choices about allocating our financial resources. By prioritizing our essential needs and distinguishing them from our wants, we can ensure that our financial decisions align with our long-term goals and values. This clarity empowers us to spend wisely, save responsibly, and lead a balanced and fulfilling life.

Remember, we can develop wise spending decisions by prioritizing needs over wants.

> *"True wisdom lies in discerning between needs and wants, for it is in prioritizing the essential over the superficial that we find lasting fulfillment. By mastering the art of wise spending, we align our choices with our values, freeing ourselves from the shackles of desire and embracing the abundance found in simplicity."*

1.3 The Power of Saving

"The power of saving money lies not only in accumulating wealth, but in mastering one's desires and finding tranquility in knowing that one possesses the means to weather life's storms."

Introduction To Saving Money For Future Goals And Emergencies

L et me tell you a secret that will help you pursue your dreams and make them come true. It's called saving money for the future! You see, saving means setting aside a little bit of money from what you have now so that you can use it later when you need it the most.

Imagine this: You have a jar, and every time you receive money, whether from your allowance or doing chores, you put a portion of it into the jar. It may seem like a small amount at first, but it grows into something big and wonderful over time. By saving your money, you create a special treasure that you can use to make your future dreams come true.

Now, think about the things you want to achieve in the future. Do you dream of going on a special trip, buying a new lacrosse stick, or even saving for college? By saving money, you are taking small steps towards these goals. It's like planting seeds and watching them grow into beautiful flowers or tall trees.

Remember, saving money requires patience and discipline. Sometimes, you might see something you want right now, like a shiny new toy, and spending your saved money on it may be tempting. But if you stay focused on your future goals and keep saving, you will be able to afford something even more special and meaningful in the long run. That's not to say you should deprive yourself of things you need now. As long as your savings are on track with your future goals, you can meet your immediate and future needs by maintaining discipline and keeping your eye on the goal.

So, my young friend, start saving today. Every little bit counts, and with time, your jar of savings will grow into a mighty treasure that will help you turn your dreams into reality. Believe in the power of saving, and you'll be amazed at what you can achieve.

One of my clients, who just so happens to be my son, Gabe, had big dreams of studying in the historic city of Rome and playing collegiate lacrosse. Gabe had a passion for fashion and a collection of vintage VHS tapes that he treasured. Every time he had some money, he couldn't resist the allure of trendy clothes and rare tapes, often prioritizing these immediate desires over saving for his future goals.

As Gabe grew older, he realized that his impulsive spending habits had hindered his ability to save for his future aspirations. He yearned to experience the rich history of Rome and play lacrosse at the collegiate level. Still, his lack of financial preparedness left him feeling discouraged.

Determined to turn his situation around, Gabe made a solemn promise to himself. He understood that saving for his future goals required discipline and sacrifice. Gabe committed to prioritizing his long-term ambitions over short-term gratification, shifting his focus from clothes and tapes to building a strong financial foundation.

With newfound determination, Gabe set up a strict budget and made a conscious effort to curb his impulsive spending. He redirected the money that would have gone towards unnecessary purchases into a dedicated savings account for his future education and lacrosse dreams in Rome.

As time went on, Gabe's dedication to saving began to pay off. His savings grew steadily, and with each passing day, his dream of studying in Rome and playing collegiate lacrosse felt closer to becoming a reality. The sacrifices he made by resisting the urge to splurge on clothes and tapes became a small price to pay for the fulfillment of his long-held aspirations.

Finally, the day arrived when Gabe received the acceptance letter to a prestigious university in Rome, offering him the opportunity to pursue his academic and athletic dreams. He was overwhelmed with gratitude and realized that his commitment to wise financial decisions had made this incredible journey possible.

Gabe's story serves as a valuable lesson in financial responsibility and prioritizing future goals. It reminds us that while immediate desires may be tempting, the long-term rewards of disciplined saving are far more significant. Gabe's determination to overcome his spending habits and achieve his dreams of studying in Rome and playing collegiate lacrosse is an inspiration to us all, showing the transformative power of financial discipline and the fulfillment that comes from pursuing our passions.

Basics Of Setting Aside Money From Earnings And Allowances

Here are five simple techniques you can use to set aside money from your earnings and allowances:

Piggy Bank Power: Get yourself a piggy bank or a special jar just for your savings. My dad always had a large jar that he would save hundreds of dollars in change and small bills that we got to count and put into coin rolls a couple times a year. Every time you receive money, whether from your allowance or doing chores, put some of it into your piggy bank. It's like feeding your savings with every coin and bill! #feedthepig

Goal Getter: Think about something you really want to save up for, like a cool toy or a fun night at the drive-in with your friends or family. Set a savings goal and decide how much money you want to save each time you get some. Then, keep saving until you reach your goal!

Divide and Conquer: Imagine your money is like a Spiros pizza. Yummy, right? Now, slice it up! Divide your money into different parts - one for spending, one for saving, and even one for sharing with others if you like. By saving a portion, you're making your money work for you!

Super Savings Account: If you're ready for a big step, ask your parents to help you open a savings account at a bank. It's like having a special place to keep your money safe and even grow over time. You can go to the bank and deposit your savings, just like a superhero!

Track Your Savings: Keep a record of how much money you save each time. You can use a notebook, a colorful chart, or a savings tracker app. Seeing your savings grow can be exciting and help you stay motivated to save even more!

Remember, my young friend, setting aside money for the future is like planting seeds. With each penny you save, you're growing a little garden of financial independence and possibilities. Using these simple techniques, you'll become a super saver and build a strong foundation for a bright and exciting future!

1.4 Setting Goals

"Goals give direction to our actions, purpose to our endeavors, and meaning to our lives."

Setting Short-Term And Long-Term Financial Goals

Setting short-term financial goals is crucial for several reasons including:

Focus and Clarity: Short-term financial goals provide focus and clarity in our financial journey. By setting specific and achievable targets, we can direct our efforts and resources toward accomplishing them. This clarity helps us stay motivated and maintain a sense of purpose in managing our finances. Think, I need to have money to buy 10 Churros on our trip to Disney World in 6 months or set a goal in January to have the money to buy that little clear backpack of fireworks for the Fourth of July Independence Day Celebration.

Building Financial Habits: Short-term goals serve

as building blocks for long-term financial success. When we set and achieve small goals, we develop positive financial habits. Whether saving a certain amount each month or paying off a small debt, these short-term goals instill discipline, responsibility, and good money management practices that lay the foundation for future financial well-being.

Measuring Progress and Celebrating Milestones: Short-term financial goals allow us to track our progress and celebrate milestones along the way. As we achieve each goal, we gain a sense of accomplishment and satisfaction, boosting our confidence and motivation to pursue larger financial objectives. These smaller victories help us stay on track and provide encouragement as we work towards our long-term financial aspirations.

So, setting short-term financial goals provides focus, helps build positive financial habits, and allows us to measure progress and celebrate achievements like saving to buy your father a Father's Day gift or your mother flowers on Mother's Day. By breaking down our financial journey into manageable steps, we increase our chances of success and create a solid framework for long-term financial well-being.

Setting **long-term** financial goals is very important for several reasons:

Vision and Direction: Long-term goals provide a clear vision and direction for our financial future. They help us define what we want to achieve in the long run, such as retiring comfortably, purchasing a home, or starting a business. A well-defined long-term goal keeps us focused and motivated, guiding our financial decisions and actions toward that desired outcome.

Financial Security and Independence: Long-term goals are essential for building financial security and independence. Setting goals prioritizing saving, and investing for the future creates a safety net that protects us from unexpected financial challenges. Long-term goals also empower us to work towards financial independence, allowing us to make choices that align with our values and aspirations.

Wealth Accumulation and Growth: Long-term financial goals allow us to accumulate wealth and foster its growth over time. By investing in stocks, bonds, or real estate, we can leverage the power of compounding and asset appreciation to steadily increase our wealth.

Setting long-term goals encourages regular saving and strategic investment decisions, which can lead to long-term financial prosperity and abundance. Setting long-term financial goals provides us with a clear vision, helps us build financial security and independence, and enables us to accumulate and grow wealth over time. Focusing on the future and making intentional choices increases our chances of achieving financial success and enjoying a fulfilling and prosperous life. To aid in making intentional choices, our short-term and long-term financial goals should be written down in a prominent place and referred to often. Making these goals into a vision for the future will help ensure success. When you get your allowance, birthday money, or money from mowing the lawn, pull out your short and long-term goals sheet and split up the money immediately. PAY YOUR FUTURE GOALS FIRST. What is left over can be used for anything you like.

The Importance Of Saving For Specific Objectives

Saving money for a specific goal is essential because it provides us with a tangible target to work towards. When we have a clear goal in mind, such as buying swag at Universal Studios, saving for a new lacrosse helmet, or saving for college, staying motivated and disciplined in our saving efforts becomes easier. Setting a goal helps us define the purpose and value of our savings, creating a sense of purpose and direction. Moreover, having a specific goal allows us to plan effectively, break down the target into manageable steps, and track our progress along the way. It helps us make intentional financial decisions, prioritize our spending, and allocate our money wisely. By setting a goal, we create a roadmap to success, increasing our chances of achieving our desired outcome and fulfilling our aspirations.

1.5 Saving Strategies

"The humble piggy bank becomes a vessel of wisdom, as each coin saved instills discipline, patience, and the transformation of desires into purposeful savings."

The Social Security Administration stated that the average income in the United States is around $60,000 annually. If we simply get into a regular and automated habit of saving just 10% of that income ($10 for every $100 we earn), we would have well over $1,000,000 at 65 or retirement age. Saving a small amount at an early age, over time, is critical to future financial success. Every little bit counts, consistency is the key.

Exploring Simple Saving Strategies Such As Piggy Banks Or Savings Jars

Two popular money-saving strategies for young people with parents supporting their "needs" to achieve short-term and long-term goals are the 10-40-50 rule and the envelope system. The 10-40-50 rule involves dividing your income into three categories: 10% for needs (such as food, clothing, and shelter), hopefully, Mom and Dad pay for most of this, 40% for wants (like toys or entertainment), and 50% for savings. This strategy helps children understand the importance of balancing spending and saving, enabling them to allocate a portion of their earnings toward their goals. Save half of what you earn, and you are nearly guaranteed to find financial success in the future.

On the other hand, the envelope system involves using different envelopes for different savings goals. You can label each envelope with a specific goal, such as "New Cleats" or "Trip to the San Diego Zoo," and allocate some of your earnings into these envelopes. This strategy teaches about saving for specific objectives and provides a visual representation of your progress. By physically seeing the money accumulate in each envelope, you can feel a sense of accomplishment and motivation to continue saving. To set up the envelope system, you only need a package of letter-size envelopes and a box to put them in. Make it fun, decorate your box, and write reminder notes to yourself on the outside of the box and the envelopes. Remind yourself what you are saving for, and have fun doing it.

Together these two strategies are foolproof. The

40% that goes toward WANTS can be broken up into multiple envelopes, Bike, Shoes, Laptop, Graphics Card, Gaming Keyboard, XBOX, whatever the WANTS goals are, you can feed each envelope every time you earn money. Some WANTS goals may be bigger than others and may get more money put toward them, but the important part is that your money is being split into NEEDS, WANTS, and SAVINGS.

Both strategies instill valuable financial habits, teaching the importance of goal-setting, budgeting, and saving. By employing these techniques, you can develop responsible money management skills and learn to make intentional choices with your finances, paving the way for a lifetime of financial success.

CHAPTER 2
BUDGETING
AND SPENDING
WISELY

"True wealth is not measured by the abundance of possessions, but by the mastery of one's desires. By practicing mindful budgeting and wise spending, we align our values with our financial choices, finding contentment in simplicity and freedom in restraint."

2.1 Creating a Budget

I want to talk to you about the importance of creating a budget. You see, a budget is like a roadmap for your finances. It helps you plan and manage your money smartly and responsibly. By creating a budget, you can track your income, know where your money is going, and ensure you have enough for your needs and wants. One of the most important things you can do to succeed in life is to ensure you always know where your money is coming from, how much, and where it is being spent. Even if you aren't great at money or paying the bills, or if you believe it is going to be your partner's job in your future relationship, simply having a solid grasp of the numbers will reduce stress, encourage open communication, and create an atmosphere where talking about money is not only not bad, it is ideal.

Having a budget gives you control over your finances and allows you to set and achieve your goals. Whether saving up for something special, paying off debts, or planning for the future, a budget is the key to making it happen. It also helps you avoid overspending and unnecessary debt, ensuring financial security and peace of mind.

Introduction To Budgeting And Its

Importance In Managing Money

A simple exercise in creating a budget.

1. Calculate Income:

Write down all sources of income, such as monthly salary from the first job and any additional earnings, like allowances or side gigs, like earnings from your lemonade stand, mowing lawns, social media influencer money, the money you may earn from releasing your music on Soundcloud, etc.

2. Track Expenses:

List all monthly expenses, including rent, utilities, groceries, transportation, entertainment, and other regular expenses. You won't have many of these as your parents take care of most of them, but it is important to figure out what you must pay for every month.

It's essential to be thorough and include both fixed expenses (like rent) and variable expenses (like fast food, in-game purchases, or shopping).

3. Categorize and Prioritize:

Organize expenses into categories, such as housing, transportation, food, entertainment, and savings.

Prioritize essential expenses, like rent and groceries, over discretionary spending. Meaning it's more important to pay the bills before buying yourself a new Oculus game.

4. Set Financial Goals:

Identify short-term and long-term financial goals, such as building an emergency fund, paying off debts, saving for a specific purchase, or investing in the future. Allocate a portion of the income towards these goals to make steady progress.

4. Create the Budget:

Based on the income and expenses, calculate the surplus (how much is left over after everything) or deficit (income minus expenses). This will be difficult if you are young without a regular income. Still, again, it is critical to understand where your money comes from and where it is going.

Adjust spending as needed to ensure income covers all essential expenses, leaving room for savings and achieving financial goals.

5. Monitor and Revise:

Regularly track spending against the budget to ensure compliance and identify areas where adjustments might be necessary. Be flexible and willing to change the budget as circumstances or financial goals evolve.

Remember, the key to successful budgeting is discipline and consistency. By creating a budget and sticking to it, you can take control of your finances and set a strong foundation for a financially secure future. Don't be afraid of budgeting; don't think it has to be some grand document or spreadsheet. Simply writing it down will help tremendously in understanding how your money is working or not working for you. Remember, you are building habits and routines that your future self will appreciate.

NOTE: Many free apps for your phone can be used to create simple budgets. These streamline the process and keep your budget at your fingertips.

Basics Of Identifying Income Sources And Allocating Funds For Different Purposes

When it comes to budgeting, identifying and allocating income sources are essential steps in creating a well-organized and effective budget. Here are some of the best ways to go about it:

Identify All Income Sources (where the money comes from):

Start by listing all sources of income, including your main salary or wages from your job. If you have multiple jobs, include them as well. Don't forget to account for any additional sources of income, such as allowances, freelance work, or any other regular earnings.

Track and Record Income:

Keep track of your income regularly. Create a system to record each payment, whether a paycheck or any other income, in a spreadsheet, a whiteboard and marker, or a budgeting app. Remember, this is an exercise in knowing where your money is coming from and how much.

Ensure that your recorded income is accurate and up-to-date, so you clearly understand how much money you have available to budget.

Categorize Your Expenses (where your money is being spent):

Group your expenses into different categories, such as food, entertainment (going to the movies, money for giant turkey legs at the State Fair, Disneyland), savings, and debt payments (money you owe somebody else). Be thorough and include all expenses, whether fixed (like your phone bill) or variable (like candy and treats that change in the amount you might buy monthly).

Prioritize Essential Expenses:

Prioritize essential expenses, which are the most important things you must spend your money on, such as your cell phone, Xbox Pass, or whatever is "necessary" for your daily living. Allocate enough funds to cover these essential expenses before considering discretionary spending or spending on items that are Wants as opposed to Needs.

Allocate Funds for Financial Goals:

Set aside a portion of your money for your financial goals, such as building an emergency fund, saving for a specific purchase, paying off debts, or investing/saving for the future. Determine how much you need to save for each goal and allocate funds accordingly. We talked about this before in the saving chapter. This can be in envelopes, custodial or varsity savings accounts at the bank, or other ways to set money aside for specific goals.

Be Realistic and Flexible:

Be realistic about your income and expenses. Don't overestimate your earnings or underestimate your spending. Being realistic will help ensure that you meet your goals. If you need more money, you can use this information from your budget to find other income through new jobs, a raise in allowance, mowing the neighborhood lawns, lemonade stand, selling stuff online, etc. Be flexible and willing to adjust your budget as needed. Life circumstances and financial goals may change, so it's essential to review and revise your budget periodically. By identifying your income sources accurately and allocating funds thoughtfully, you can create a budget that aligns with your financial goals and helps you manage your money effectively. Budgeting empowers you to make informed financial decisions, avoid overspending, and work towards achieving your financial aspirations.

2.2 Tracking Expenses

"In the art of self-mastery, our mind must keep a vigilant watch over the coin's journey, tracing the path of each expenditure with unwavering scrutiny. By tracking expenses, we uncover the essence of our desires, separating needs from wants, and reclaiming dominion over our financial realm. With each entry inscribed, we gain the wisdom to discern between the fleeting pleasures of indulgence and the enduring fulfillment of responsible stewardship. In the ledger of our lives, tracking expenses becomes the philosopher's compass, guiding us towards the harmony of financial virtue and the mastery of our own destiny."

Importance Of Keeping Track Of Your Spending

Let's discuss why tracking your expenses is supercritical. You know, it's like being a money detective! When you follow your expenses, you get a clear picture of where your money is going. It helps you see how much you spend on food, clothes, and fun activities. By keeping tabs on your spending, you can figure out if you're using your money wisely or if there are places where you can cut back.

Tracking expenses also helps you stick to your budget and achieve your financial goals. When you know where your money is going, you can make smarter decisions about saving and investing. Plus, it's a great way to learn more about your spending habits and become more responsible with your money. So, grab a pen and paper or use an excellent budgeting app, and let's start tracking those expenses like a pro!
You'll be amazed at how much it can help you take control of your money and make it work for you!

Identifying Common Spending Categories And Tracking Money In And Out

As a teenager, you may find yourself spending money on various things that are important to you. Here are three common spending categories for teenagers and some tips on tracking your money in and out:

Entertainment and Social Activities:

This includes expenses like going to the movies, dining out with friends, or attending concerts and events. To track your spending, record each outing or activity and how much you spend on tickets, food, and other expenses related to the event.

Clothing and Personal Style:

Clothing and personal style are a massive factor in the pre-and teenage years. It is a significant way we express ourselves and tell a bit of our story to those around us. This category includes expenses like buying new GAP-Supreme-Banana Republic-Hot Topic, Doc Martins-Converse-Nikes, belts to match your shoes, necklaces, watches, earrings, and grooming products like skin care, razors or shampoos and perfumes.

To track your spending, list each clothing purchase and how much you spent on each item. This will help you see how much you allocate to your style.

Technology and Gadgets:

Keeping up with the latest technology is very important, such as smartphones, VR headsets, or video games. This category includes expenses related to purchasing or upgrading electronic devices and games.

To track your spending, write down each tech-related purchase and how much you spent. This will help you understand how much of your money goes toward technology. You can use a simple budgeting notebook, a spreadsheet, or a budgeting app on your phone to track your money in and out effectively. Regularly update your spending records and compare them to your income or allowance to see how much you're saving or if you need to adjust your spending in any category. By tracking your expenses, you'll gain valuable insights into your spending habits and be able to make informed decisions about how to manage your money wisely.

2.3 Needs vs. Wants
in Spending

"The essence of rational spending lies in the unyielding pursuit of needs over wants. It is through the discerning mind that one grasps the significance of distinguishing between the essentials that sustain life and the fleeting desires that enslave it. To prioritize needs is to embrace the sovereignty of one's values, aligning spending with the pursuit of true self-interest and the realization of a flourishing existence."

Reinforcing The Concept Of Prioritizing Needs Over Wants When Making Spending Decisions

As a teenager, learning to prioritize needs over wants when making spending decisions is a crucial lesson in building a solid financial foundation. It is natural to be drawn to the allure of trendy gadgets, fashionable clothes, and exciting entertainment, but understanding the difference between "needs and wants" empowers you to make responsible choices. By focusing on your needs first, such as food, shelter, education, and essential personal care, you ensure that your fundamental requirements are met before indulging in discretionary purchases.

Reinforcing the concept of prioritizing needs over wants helps you develop discipline and self-control, essential traits for financial success in the long run. It teaches you the value of delayed gratification, understanding that you can secure a more prosperous future by forgoing impulsive wants today (remember Gabe's story). Balancing your spending decisions rationally allows you to allocate funds wisely, creating opportunities to save for important goals, such as a college education or pursuing your passions.

Moreover, prioritizing needs over wants cultivates an appreciation for the intrinsic worth of non-material aspects of life. By focusing on your necessities, you nurture your personal growth, relationships, and experiences contributing to lasting fulfillment and well-being. In embracing this philosophy, you free yourself from the grasp of excess consumerism, finding contentment in the pursuit of genuine needs and the quest for meaningful endeavors that align with your authentic self. Remember, by mastering the art of prioritizing needs over wants, you forge a path toward financial wisdom and a life of purposeful abundance.

Thoughtful And Mindful Spending Habits

Thoughtful and mindful spending habits are a transformative approach that empowers individuals to make conscious and responsible financial decisions. By cultivating awareness around spending choices, we can develop a deeper understanding of the impact of our purchases on overall financial well-being and long-term goals. Thoughtful spending involves considering the value and necessity of each expense, weighing its significance against other priorities, and making choices that align with our values and aspirations.

Mindful spending goes beyond impulse purchases and quick fixes. It involves pausing to reflect on the needs and desires behind each spending decision, recognizing the potential consequences, and making deliberate choices that foster financial prudence. Developing mindful spending habits as a teenager will equip you with the tools to resist peer pressure, marketing tactics, and societal expectations. It will empower you to make independent choices that serve your best interests.

By fostering thoughtful and mindful spending habits, you develop a sense of financial empowerment, taking charge of your financial destinies. You learn to distinguish between momentary gratification and long-term fulfillment, sowing the seeds of financial success early in life. Mindful spending ensures a stable financial future and fosters a sense of contentment and self-assurance.

2.4 Smart Shopping

Smart shopping is a savvy money management approach that involves maximizing value for money and avoiding impulse purchases and overspending. By prioritizing value, individuals can make well-informed decisions, compare prices, seek discounts, and ensure that their hard-earned money is spent wisely on high-quality products or services. Additionally, practicing restraint against impulsive buying helps to maintain financial discipline, as it allows time for thoughtful consideration before making a purchase. This mindful approach prevents wasteful spending, keeps budgets in check, and ensures that financial resources are directed toward fulfilling essential needs and achieving long-term financial goals. Smart shopping empowers individuals to make intentional choices with their money, optimizing its potential and promoting responsible financial habits for a secure and prosperous future.

Introducing The Idea Of Comparison Shopping And Seeking Value For Money

Let's talk about an incredible money-saving skill called comparison shopping. Imagine you're looking to buy a new iPhone or a cool pair of Nikes. Instead of rushing to the first store you see or buying from the sneakerhead in gym class, comparison shopping is about taking a little extra time to explore different options and find the best value for your money. It's like being an intelligent detective in the shopping world!

Here's how it works: First, list the things you want to buy and the essential features. Then, check out different stores or websites to see what they offer. Compare prices, read reviews from other customers, and remember to consider any discounts or special deals. By doing this, you can find the best deal that matches your desire.

Regarding sites like Amazon or other online shopping portals, Comparison shopping is crucial because it can save you time and money and ensure you make informed purchase decisions. With millions of products available on Amazon and other sites, it's easy to get overwhelmed by the options. By comparing similar products from different sellers, you can find the best price and quality that suits your needs.

Reading customer reviews and ratings lets you gain insights from real users, helping you assess the product's performance and reliability. Additionally, Amazon offers various deals and discounts, and comparing prices can help you snag the best deal available. Comparison shopping lets you ensure you're not paying too much for something and gets you the most bang for your buck. So, next time you're shopping, take a deep breath, do some detective work, and you'll be amazed at how much you can save and the cool stuff you'll find!

Understanding The Importance Of Evaluating Quality, Price, And Usefulness Before Making Purchases

As young people embark on their money management journey, considering quality, price, and effectiveness is incredibly important. Let me break it down for you.

Firstly, thinking about the quality of a product ensures that you are getting something that will last and won't need frequent replacements. Investing in higher-quality items might cost more upfront, but it can save you money in the long run because you won't have to buy a new one soon after. I like to employ the middle-to-high technique in purchasing. The low-end product may be ok in some scenarios. However, you will be far happier in the long run if you choose quality over price. So long as the quality is better at a higher price, doing your homework comes into play.

Next, considering cost is crucial because you want to ensure you spend your money wisely. Comparing prices of similar products helps you find the best deal and prevents overspending on something overpriced. Being mindful of your budget and getting the best value for your money is essential as you start managing your finances.

Lastly, considering usefulness means considering how much you will use or benefit from a purchase. Avoid buying things impulsively that might end up sitting in your room untouched. Instead, focus on items that serve a purpose in your life or contribute to your goals and interests.

So, when you combine these factors and make thoughtful decisions based on quality, price, and usefulness, you'll become a savvy shopper and a master of your money management journey. By being mindful of your spending, you can make your money work for you and set a solid foundation for financial success in the future!

2.5 Delayed Gratification

"The wise embrace delayed gratification, recognizing that patience and self-discipline sow the seeds of enduring fulfillment."

Delayed gratification refers to the practice of postponing immediate rewards or pleasures in favor of long-term benefits or goals. It involves exercising self-discipline and patience by resisting the temptation to indulge in instant gratification and making choices that prioritize future rewards or outcomes instead. By embracing delayed gratification, you can learn to forgo short-term pleasures or desires in pursuing more significant achievements, whether saving money for a specific goal, studying diligently for future success, or adopting healthy habits to improve overall well-being. This concept emphasizes the value of long-term planning and self-control, enabling individuals to make wiser decisions that lead to more profound and lasting rewards in their lives.

The Value Of Patience And Waiting

Before Making Impulse Purchases

Let's talk about a young man named Alex, a client of mine in the past. Alex had always been impulsive when spending money, especially on big-ticket items. He loved the thrill of instant gratification and often indulged in impulse purchases without considering the long-term consequences.

One day, while in Coast Guard training school in California, Alex came across a silver Toyota 4Runner at a car dealership. It was love at first sight. Without a second thought and against his father's advice, he decided to buy the car impulsively, believing it would symbolize his success and status. Despite the excitement of driving this beautiful new SUV, reality quickly set in when the monthly payments started to pile up.

As time passed, Alex realized that the car loan was more than he could afford. The financial burden weighed heavily on him, and he struggled with other expenses. He had less money to save, and his daily needs became challenging. The 4Runner, once a source of pride, became a constant reminder of the consequences of his impulsive decisions.

Feeling overwhelmed, Alex sought help from a financial advisor who encouraged him to reevaluate his priorities and create a budget to manage his money more responsibly. Together, they worked on a plan to improve his financial situation, which included getting a second job to increase monthly cash flow. With patience and determination, Alex committed to making more thoughtful spending choices and avoiding impulse purchases.

As he consistently tried to budget wisely and prioritize saving, Alex's financial situation improved. He learned the value of waiting before making big decisions and the importance of considering the long-term impact of his choices. Eventually, he could pay off his car loan, easing his financial burden and allowing him to regain control of his finances.

Through this challenging experience, Alex transformed into a more patient and responsible individual. He became a shining example of how practicing patience and waiting before making impulse purchases can lead to financial stability and peace of mind. With his newfound wisdom, Alex embraced a more mindful approach to money management, ensuring a brighter and more secure financial future.

Of course, there was no Alex; Alex was me. And did I seek the advice of a financial advisor at the age of 21? I did not. I did, however, realize the error in my judgment once I realized that I could barely afford to put food on my table and pay for my apartment and sweet new 4Runner. I dug out of the situation by tightening the belt. I ultimately paid off the 4Runner, in 6 years, which was a greater sense of pride than the purchase or even the car itself. This serious event took me to open my eyes to the power of thinking before purchasing and delaying gratification.

Promoting Responsible Decision-Making By Considering Long-Term Consequences

Let's talk about the importance of responsible decision-making and how it can significantly shape your future. Every choice you make has consequences, not just for today but for the long term. By making thoughtful decisions now, you can pave the way for a brighter and more fulfilling life.

Consider your dreams and aspirations: perhaps you dream of going to college, owning a home, or starting a family one day. Well, guess what? Responsible decision-making plays a key role in turning those dreams into reality. You can build a strong financial foundation by being mindful of your spending and saving wisely. That means you'll be better prepared to afford college tuition, purchase a home, and provide a stable environment for your future family.

Think of it as planting seeds today for a beautiful garden tomorrow. When you make decisions with the long term in mind, you're sowing the seeds of financial security, independence, and success. So, before you make any big choices or spend your money, take a moment to consider the long-term consequences. Ask yourself, "Will this decision help me achieve my dreams? Will it lead to a better future?" By doing so, you'll be well on your way to making a world of difference in your life and setting yourself up for an extraordinary journey!

CHAPTER 3
BANKING AND
FINANCIAL
INSTITUTIONS

"Banks stand as a bastion of financial prudence, safeguarding the fruits of labor with unwavering fidelity. Through their timeless halls, they fortify the virtue of patience, gathering the streams of wealth, and cultivating the strength of compound growth. With each coin entrusted, banks become sentinels of fortitude, empowering individuals to transcend the fleeting desires of the present for the abundant rewards of the future."

3.1 Banks

Banks are like trustworthy guardians for your hard-earned money. When you put your money in a bank, it stays safe and secure, protected from the risks of keeping it all in your room or wallet. Plus, banks offer many cool services like savings accounts, checking accounts, and even interest on your savings! With a bank account, you can learn the power of saving and watch your money grow.

Opening your first bank account is an exciting step towards financial independence. It's like having your own money headquarters, where you can deposit your allowance, pay for things electronically, and even get a debit card to shop online or in stores. Having a bank account also teaches you how to manage your money responsibly. You'll learn to keep track of your transactions, check your balances, and maybe even set up automatic savings transfers to reach your financial goals faster!

How do banks make money, you ask? Simple, Banks make money on our investments through various mechanisms, primarily as intermediaries between savers and borrowers. When we deposit money into a bank account, the bank pools these funds together and lends them to other customers as loans. The interest charged on these loans is higher than the interest paid to savers, allowing banks to generate profit from the spread, known as the "interest rate spread."

Additionally, banks offer investment products such as certificates of deposit (CDs) and mutual funds, where customers can invest their money for a specific period or in diversified portfolios. These investment products often come with fees or management charges, contributing to the bank's revenue.

Furthermore, banks may invest their capital in various financial instruments, such as stocks, bonds, and government securities. The returns on these investments add to the bank's earnings.

It's important to note that banks also play a crucial role in facilitating various financial transactions, often with service fees. They provide payment processing services, offer credit cards, and engage in foreign exchange transactions, contributing to their revenue streams.

Overall, by channeling funds from savers to borrowers, offering investment products, and engaging in financial transactions, banks can earn profits and sustain their operations while serving the financial needs of individuals and businesses. How banks make money isn't the point of this book, but it is important to understand how money works and how it is moving through the world.

Remember, when choosing a bank, look for one that offers no fees, good customer service, and maybe even a special account for students like you. Look into your local credit unions or where your parent's bank accounts are set up. Often, your parents can open an account that is linked to their account, which can help in the management of the account as well as transferring money like allowances. Take this opportunity to learn about the different banking options and how they can help you become a smart and savvy saver. So, opening your bank account is the first step towards financial empowerment. It's a journey worth embarking upon, and it'll set you on the path to financial success and freedom!

Understanding The Role Of Banks In Keeping Money Safe And Offering Financial Services

So, what can a bank do for you. You likely already have a decent concept of what banks accomplish, but let's talk about it anyway. Think of a bank as a super secure vault for your money. When you deposit your cash in a bank, they keep it safe and sound, so you don't have to worry about losing it or having it stolen. It's like having your own personal money superhero!

But that's not all banks can do. They offer a bunch of fantastic financial services too! With a savings account, you can watch your money grow because the bank pays you interest. It's like a bonus for keeping your money with them. It doesn't pay a ton, but as time goes by and more money is saved, it will continue to compound, and in the long run, you will see real growth. Plus, banks can help you manage your money better with a checking account. You can use a debit card to buy stuff online or in stores, and the bank keeps track of all your transactions, so you know exactly how much you have left to spend.

Banks can even help you achieve big goals, like buying a car or going to college. They can lend you money through loans, which you can repay over time. It's like having a helping hand when you need it most. However, loans or credit should be used conservatively, as paying cash for an item is ideal. So, the next time you think about keeping your money safe or need financial superpowers, remember that banks are here to help you make the most of your money journey!

Basic Knowledge Of Banking Products,

Such As Savings Accounts, Piggy Banks, And Investment Accounts

Checking Accounts:

- Thee are your most common and necessary types of accounts.
- Checking accounts come with a debit card for you to use in   stores and online
- They also track your money-in (deposits) and money-out (spending).

Savings Accounts:
- A savings account is a safe place to keep your money in a bank.
- It helps you earn interest on your savings, meaning your money can grow over time.
- You can deposit or withdraw money from a savings account whenever you need to. Still, some banks may have restrictions on the number of withdrawals.

Investment Accounts:
- Investment accounts are for growing your money through investments like stocks, bonds, or mutual funds. We will talk more about investments later.
- They have the potential for higher returns but also come with some risk, from very high risk where you could lose all your money, or relatively low risk where your returns (kind of like interest)

aren't as high. Still, you don't risk losing all of your investment.

- It's important to research and understand different investment options before making decisions.

Remember, banks are here to help you manage your money and achieve your financial goals. Savings and piggy banks are great for short-term savings, while investment accounts can be used for long-term growth. As you learn more about banking products, you'll become a money-savvy individual with the tools to make the most of your hard-earned cash!

Opening a traditional bank account as a minor involves specific steps and considerations. Each bank will be slightly different; however, here's a general guide:

1. Choose the Right Bank: Research different banks and compare their offerings, fees, and benefits to find one that suits your needs.

2. Check Age Requirements: Ensure the bank allows minors to open accounts and check the minimum age required.

3. Parental Consent: Since you are a minor, you'll need a parent or legal guardian to co-sign on the account.

4. Gather Identification: You'll typically need

identification documents, such as your birth certificate, social security number, and a government-issued ID.

5. Visit the Bank: Go to the bank branch with your parent or guardian to initiate the account opening process.

6. Complete the Application: Fill out the necessary forms and provide all the required information.

7. Set Funding: Decide how you'll fund the account, whether by depositing or transferring money from another account.

8. Discuss Account Type: Speak with a bank representative to select the appropriate account type, such as a savings or checking account.

9. Review Terms and Conditions: Ensure you and your parent or guardian understand the account's terms, fees, and features. If you don't understand something, ASK; they are there to serve you.

10. Get Your Debit Card: If applicable, discuss obtaining a debit card linked to your account for easier access.

Remember, each bank may have specific requirements or procedures, so it's best to contact the bank or go online and read through their requirements beforehand to confirm their policies for opening accounts for minors. With your parent or guardian's support and understanding, you'll be on your way to managing your bank account responsibly and taking your first steps toward financial independence.

3.2 Saving and Interest

"Saving money becomes a masterful art, for in the patient accumulation of wealth lies the seed of enduring prosperity. As interest blooms upon the soil of one's savings, the saver witnesses the harmonious dance of patience and growth, reaping the rewards of steadfastness and foresight."

Explaining The Concept Of Interest And How It Helps Money Grow

Interest is like the gentle rain that nourishes the seeds of your savings, causing them to grow into a flourishing garden of wealth. When you deposit your money in a savings account or invest it, the bank or financial institution rewards your prudence with a little extra bonus, known as interest. This bonus is a percentage of your saved money, calculated over time. As the days turn into months and the months into years, the interest keeps adding up, making your savings or investments grow steadily.

Here's the magical part: as your savings grow, the interest starts to work on the increased amount, creating a snowball effect. This compounding interest becomes a powerful ally, allowing your money to grow even faster. The longer you keep your money invested or saved, the more significant the impact of compounding interest becomes.

So, with the magic of interest and some patience, your money can grow and multiply, helping you reach your financial goals and ensuring a more prosperous future. Embrace the power of interest, and you'll witness the enchanting dance of wealth and abundance unfold.

Introducing The Idea Of Compound Interest And Its Benefits Over Time

Compound interest is like a magician's trick that makes your money grow exponentially over time. Unlike simple interest, which only calculates interest on the initial amount you put in the account, compound interest considers both the principal (the original amount) and the accumulated interest from previous periods. As a result, each time the interest is added to your savings or investment, the total amount increases, and the subsequent interest calculation becomes larger. This creates a compounding effect that accelerates your money's growth over the long term.

The beauty of compound interest lies in its snowballing nature. As time passes, the interest in your savings or investments grows larger and larger, fueling even more growth. It's like a never-ending cycle of multiplying your money. The more time you give compound interest to work its magic, the greater the benefits. Compound interest is compelling for long-term savings or investments, such as retirement or education funds.

I had the pleasure of advising a young man named Sam, who was eager to start saving money for his future. Sam had just landed his first job and wanted to make the most of his hard-earned income. He was excited about the prospect of saving but needed to figure out where to begin.

I sat down with Sam and explained the power of compound interest. I told him how he could watch his money grow exponentially over time by putting aside a portion of his earnings regularly. At first, Sam was intrigued but skeptical. He wondered if such a simple concept could really make a difference.

Encouraged by my guidance, Sam started small, setting up monthly automatic transfers to his savings account. As the months passed, he was astonished to witness the magic of compound interest at work. He saw his savings increase from his contributions and the interest earned on his growing balance.

Sam became more and more enthusiastic about saving. He started increasing the amount he set aside, realizing that the more he saved, the more he benefited from compound interest's powerful effect. The numbers spoke for themselves, and Sam's confidence in his financial future grew daily.

Over time, Sam learned that patience and consistency were the keys to unlocking the full potential of compound interest. As he continued to save diligently, he was delighted to see his savings snowball into a sum he had never imagined possible.

Through this journey, Sam discovered the true magic of compound interest. What had initially seemed like a simple concept had turned into a life-changing revelation. Sam's newfound understanding of the power of saving and compound interest set him on a path to financial security and a future filled with possibility. And so, with the guidance of a wise advisor and a belief in the magic of compound interest, Sam's financial journey began, forever shaping his life in ways he could have never foreseen.

The key is to start early, be patient, and let time work wonders. Compound interest is a loyal ally, rewarding your prudence and foresight with a bountiful harvest of wealth and financial security in the coming years.

3.3 Banking Services

Banking services are like a cornucopia of financial tools and assistance at your fingertips. When you open an account with a bank, you gain access to various services designed to make managing your money more straightforward and convenient. From simple savings and checking accounts that keep your cash safe to the marvels of online banking that let you manage your finances from the comfort of your home, banking services empower you to take control of your financial journey. Need to pay bills, transfer money, or get a loan? Banks have got you covered! Whether you're saving for a dream vacation or planning for your future, banking services offer a world of possibilities to help you achieve your financial goals and make your money work for you.

Overview Of Different Services Provided By Banks, Such As Atm Usage And Online Banking

Banks play a crucial role in offering a wide array of financial services to cater to the diverse needs of their customers. One of the most convenient services is ATM usage, which allows customers to access their accounts and perform various transactions, such as cash withdrawals, balance inquiries, and fund transfers, at any time of the day or night. Online banking is another valuable service banks provide, offering customers the flexibility to manage their finances from the comfort of their homes or on the go. Through secure Internet banking platforms, users can check account balances, review transaction history, pay bills, transfer funds, and even set up automatic payments. These services provide a seamless and efficient banking experience, empowering customers to stay in control of their finances and efficiently carry out transactions.

Additionally, banks offer various savings and checking accounts, investment services, loans, credit cards, foreign currency exchange, and safety deposit boxes to meet the diverse financial needs of individuals and businesses. Overall, the range of services banks provide ensures that customers have the tools and resources to manage their money wisely and achieve their financial goals.

Emphasizing The Importance Of Security And Protecting Personal Information

The importance of security and safeguarding

personal identity cannot be overstated in today's digital age. Our personal information, such as social security numbers, bank account details, and passwords, is like a precious treasure that must be safeguarded at all costs. Identity theft and cybercrimes are on the rise, and malicious actors constantly seek ways to exploit vulnerabilities in our digital lives. By prioritizing security, we shield ourselves from potential financial ruin, emotional distress, and reputational damage from identity theft.

Protecting personal identity extends beyond the digital realm. We should safeguard physical documents like passports, driver's licenses, and credit cards in our daily lives. Simple actions, such as shredding sensitive paperwork and being cautious about sharing personal information with strangers, can go a long way in preventing identity theft.

Additionally, practicing cybersecurity measures is crucial when using digital platforms. Utilizing strong and unique passwords for each online account, enabling two-factor authentication, and avoiding suspicious links and emails can help prevent unauthorized access to our personal information. Staying vigilant and regularly monitoring financial statements for unusual activities can help detect potential security breaches early on. This is where budgeting and tracking your money movement comes into play. Know the path of each of your coins, and you will never be caught off-guard.

In a world where data breaches and cybercrimes have become commonplace, protecting personal identity is not just a matter of convenience but survival. By proactively safeguarding our personal information, we control our digital and real-world security, ensuring a safer and more secure future for ourselves and our loved ones. Remember, our identities are valuable assets, and with the proper security measures, we can preserve their sanctity and enjoy peace of mind in an increasingly interconnected world.

3.4 Responsible Borrowing

"Responsible borrowing stands as a prudent virtue, for it is the art of borrowing only that which we can repay with honor. By exercising restraint and foresight, we shield ourselves from the shackles of debt and preserve our financial freedom, ensuring that our actions remain in harmony with our values and principles."

Teaching The Basics Of Borrowing Money Responsibly

I had the privilege of working with a remarkable client named Sarah. She was a determined young woman with dreams of pursuing higher education to become a doctor. Like many aspiring students, Sarah faced the daunting prospect of paying for her college education.

Sarah sought my advice on managing the cost of her education responsibly. We delved into the concept of responsible borrowing, where she could take out student loans to cover tuition and other essential expenses while being mindful of her ability to repay them in the future. We discussed the benefits of borrowing for significant costs, such as education. Responsible borrowing could provide Sarah the means to achieve her dreams without sacrificing her financial stability. By borrowing wisely, she could focus on her studies and invest in her future without immediate financial stress.

However, I also stressed the importance of understanding the risks of borrowing. Borrowed money comes with a price—the interest that accumulates over time. Sarah needed to weigh the potential costs and obligations of taking out loans against the benefits of her education and future career opportunities. Together, we carefully planned Sarah's borrowing strategy, ensuring she borrowed only what she truly needed, and explored scholarship options and part-time work opportunities to reduce her loan amount. I emphasized the significance of making regular, on-time payments and managing her finances responsibly to avoid falling into a cycle of debt. As the years passed, Sarah embraced the wisdom of responsible borrowing and successfully completed her medical degree. With a clear understanding of the potential pitfalls of borrowing and the discipline to manage her finances diligently, she navigated through her loans responsibly, securing a bright future free from the burden of overwhelming debt.

Sarah's journey exemplified the importance of responsible borrowing. This thoughtful approach allowed her to seize opportunities and achieve her aspirations without compromising her financial well-being. It served as a testament to the power of making informed financial decisions. I felt privileged to have played a small part in guiding her toward a secure and prosperous future.

Introducing The Concept Of Loans And Emphasizing The Need To Repay Borrowed Funds

Loans can be a valuable tool to help you achieve your dreams, whether going to college, starting a business, or buying a car. They provide you with the funds you need to make big things happen! But remember, as we discussed in previous sections, borrowing money comes with responsibilities.

When you take out a loan, you promise to repay the money you borrowed, plus some extra called interest. Repaying your loans on time is crucial because it shows you're responsible and trustworthy. It also helps you build a positive credit history (known as your credit score), which is like a report card for how you handle your money. Good credit will come in handy later when you want to rent an apartment, buy a car, or even get a credit card.

Missing loan payments or paying them late can hurt your credit score and make it harder to borrow money in the future. It can also lead to extra fees and penalties, making it even more challenging to get back on track. So, when you take out a loan, create a budget to ensure you can make the payments on time. Stay organized and set reminders for due dates. If you're having trouble making a payment, don't ignore it! Reach out to your lender and discuss your situation. They might be able to help you with a repayment plan.

In the world of finances, being responsible with loans is like a superpower! By repaying your loans on time, you show that you're a reliable borrower and set yourself up for a brighter financial future. So, embrace this responsibility, and manage your loans wisely.

3.5 Giving Back

I had a client named John, who was an excellent representation of the importance of giving. John was a successful engineer with a big heart and a passion for giving back to his community. One day, as we were discussing his financial goals, John revealed his desire to support local sports organizations and positively impact young athletes' lives.

John had always been a sports enthusiast, and he saw the value that team sports brought to the lives of young people. He wanted to ensure that all children in the community could experience the joy and camaraderie of playing sports, regardless of their financial circumstances. With a heart full of determination, John began donating generously to local youth sports organizations. His contributions helped provide equipment, uniforms, and facilities, allowing young athletes to shine on the field and the court. But John didn't stop there; he wanted to be part of the journey firsthand.

Drawing from his business knowledge and experience, John decided to get actively involved. He volunteered his time to help coach young athletes, sharing his passion for sports and mentoring them to become not only skilled players but also responsible individuals. His presence on the field and the sidelines brought a sense of enthusiasm and inspiration to the players and their families. John's impact didn't end with coaching; he also joined the board of directors for the youth sports organization. He helped strategize and implement growth initiatives using his business acumen, leading to more funding and expanded programs. Under his guidance, the organization flourished, and more children were allowed to experience the transformative power of sports.

As John immersed himself in his philanthropic efforts, he discovered an incredible sense of community pride. The connections he formed with young athletes, fellow coaches, and parents were deeply meaningful. The shared sense of purpose and passion for helping others fostered a strong bond within the community. John saw firsthand how his contributions were making a lasting difference in the lives of the youth, instilling confidence, discipline, and valuable life skills.

John's story taught me that charitable giving isn't just about writing a check; it's about being actively involved and making a hands-on impact. By giving not only his financial resources but also his time and expertise, John experienced the true joy of philanthropy—a sense of community pride that came from nurturing the potential of the next generation and witnessing their growth and success. His journey exemplified the transformative power of giving, not just for those who receive but also for the giver.

Charitable Giving And The Importance Of Helping Others

More about the incredible power of charitable giving and why it's essential to help others. When we engage in acts of kindness and support, we create a ripple effect of positivity that brightens someone else's day and brings joy and fulfillment to our lives. So, let's dive into the world of charitable giving and explore how we can make a difference in the lives of others.

Firstly, charitable giving isn't just about donating money; it's about sharing our time, talents, and compassion with those in need. Whether volunteering like John in a community-based youth sports organization, at a local shelter, participating in community cleanups, or helping a friend in tough times, each act of kindness makes a significant impact. Helping others creates a sense of unity and empathy within our communities, bringing us closer together and making the world a brighter place.

Secondly, consider the issues you're passionate about and explore charitable organizations that align with those causes. Whether it's supporting environmental initiatives, advocating for animal welfare, or aiding children's education, there's a cause out there that will resonate with your heart. Get involved, learn about your contributions' impact, and witness the change you can create firsthand. Together, we can build a world where kindness and compassion are the guiding principles, strengthening and connecting our communities.

Lastly, remember that giving back isn't just about the immediate impact—it's about building a sense of fulfillment and purpose in our lives. Helping others brings a unique sense of joy and gratitude, knowing we can make a positive difference. It's about recognizing our strength to be agents of change, regardless of age or background. So, let's take on the challenge of spreading kindness and generosity, for in doing so, we not only brighten someone else's world but also find our hearts glowing with the warmth of compassion and love. Let's make a difference and create a better future for all!

CHAPTER 4
PLANNING FOR
THE FUTURE

"While planning for the future is wise, we must hold it gently in our minds, for the future remains but a realm of possibilities, not certainties."

4.1 Setting Financial Goals

One of my clients had a son named Lukas. He was an avid gamer and had his heart set on purchasing a powerful VR gaming computer to elevate his gaming experience. However, the computer he desired was quite expensive, as it had some pretty high-end components, such as a GeForce RTX 4070 Ti graphics card and a ton of RAM. He knew he needed to find a way to afford it.

One day, he overheard his parents discussing setting financial goals and how they helped them achieve their dreams. Intrigued, Lukas approached his parents and asked them to teach him about setting financial goals. They were delighted to see their son interested in responsible money management.

Together, they sat down and made a plan. Lukas decided to save a portion of his weekly allowance and any money he received from doing chores, mowing the lawn, and other jobs for his parents and grandparents. He also set a target date by which he wanted to buy the gaming computer. Each week, he diligently added his savings to a jar, keeping track of his progress with excitement.

As the days passed, Lukas realized that setting financial goals was about saving money and staying disciplined and focused on his objective. He resisted the temptation to spend his savings on other things, reminding himself of the gaming computer that awaited him at the end of his journey.

Finally, the day arrived when Lukas had saved enough money to buy the gaming computer. With a proud smile, he popped online and made the purchase he had been dreaming about for months. As he set up his new system at home, he knew that achieving this goal was just the beginning of his financial journey.

From that day forward, Lukas continued to set new financial goals for himself. He learned that he could turn his dreams into reality with determination, planning, and perseverance. As he grew older, he became wiser in managing his money, and the lessons he learned about setting financial goals became a valuable foundation for a lifetime of financial success.

Setting Financial Goals For The Future Is Super Important

Setting goals is essential for future success because it provides direction, purpose, and motivation for our actions and endeavors. Goals act as guiding stars, pointing us toward the destination we wish to reach, allowing us to chart a clear path amidst life's complexities. When I was in the Coast Guard many years ago, I was offered some leadership classes and training, which I leveraged into my time at Scottrade Financial Services, where I was rewarded with a mentorship and leadership training program with the firm. We learned an important lesson, when we set specific, measurable, achievable, relevant, and time-bound (SMART) goals, we create a roadmap that empowers us to stay focused and committed to our aspirations.

Goals also serve as powerful motivators. They fuel our determination and drive, igniting a sense of purpose that propels us forward even in the face of challenges and setbacks. By defining our goals, we clarify what truly matters to us, enabling us to effectively prioritize and allocate our time, energy, and resources.

Furthermore, setting goals helps us measure progress and celebrate achievements. As we attain milestones on our journey, we gain a sense of accomplishment and fulfillment, reinforcing our confidence and belief in our capabilities. This positive reinforcement encourages us to persevere, setting a cycle of success in motion.

Setting goals aligns with living a life of virtue and

wisdom. By consciously striving for meaningful objectives, we cultivate the art of living deliberately and with purpose, becoming the architects of our destinies. Additionally, it's important to make our goals known. Write them down, put them on a whiteboard or the lock screen on your phone. Let others know your goals, as putting your goals out into the world can be a powerful step in manifesting success. Think of being vocal and manifesting your goals, like having a friend who works on cars or tattoos. If we know what others around us are good at or want to offer to the world, we are more likely to recommend somebody go see them if they have that specific need. Like our goals, if we tell others what we are trying to do, others can help us if they find the opportunity. Nothing can be gained by keeping your goals, dreams, and aspirations private.

The Benefits Of Planning For College, Future Careers, And Big-Ticket Purchases

So there are incredible benefits to planning for college, future careers, and big-ticket purchases. While it might seem far-off, thinking ahead and setting goals now can profoundly impact your future.

Firstly, let's focus on college planning. Planning for college early on allows you to explore different options, discover your passions, and tailor your education accordingly. By researching potential colleges, scholarships, and financial aid opportunities, you can pave the way for a smoother transition into higher education and reduce the burden of student debt in the long run. If you plan on attending a specific school, look up the scholarship opportunities at the school and apply to as many of them as possible. Many scholarships go underused just because students don't take the time to write an essay or fill out their applications. Your future self will thank you for filling out these applications, as reducing student loans/debt is critical for building future wealth. Planning also helps you stay on track academically, ensuring you have the grades and extracurricular experiences that colleges value.

Next, let's dive into future career planning. Knowing your career interests and aspirations early on lets you make informed decisions about your educational path and skill development. By exploring internships, part-time jobs, or volunteering in fields of interest, you gain valuable real-world experience and build a network of contacts. Planning for your future career means setting stepping stones to success, making it more likely for you to land your dream job and excel in your chosen field.

Now, let's consider big-ticket purchases. Planning ahead is crucial, whether it's a car, a home, or significant investment. Understanding your financial goals and creating a budget will help you save and manage your money wisely. By planning for major purchases, you can avoid impulsive decisions and ensure your choices align with your long-term aspirations and financial security.

Remember that planning isn't about rigidly dictating your future. It's about setting a roadmap that allows you the flexibility to adapt and grow. By taking the time to plan for college, future careers, and big-ticket purchases, you're investing in yourself and empowering your journey toward success and fulfillment. So, embrace the power of planning, and watch as your dreams take shape, one step at a time!

4.2 Introduction to Investing

Now, we will explore the exciting world of investing—a path that can pave the way for financial growth and security. Investing is like planting seeds that grow into fruitful trees over time. So, let's embark on this journey of discovery and learn about the basics of investing.

Investing is all about putting your money to work with the goal of earning a return or profit. Instead of letting your money sit idle in a piggy bank or earning a lower rate in a savings account, investing allows you to grow your wealth and build a strong financial foundation for your future. One of the most common investment vehicles is the stock market. When you invest in stocks, you become a partial owner of a company. As the company thrives, the value of your shares increases, and you can sell them for a profit. The stock market might seem intimidating, but it's a place of opportunity and growth, where companies evolve and innovation drives progress.

Another form of investment is bonds. Bonds are like IOUs issued by governments or corporations. When you invest in bonds, you're essentially lending money to these entities, and they pay you interest over time. Bonds are generally considered more stable than stocks, making them a safer option for investors looking for consistent returns, albeit at a potentially lower level.

Additionally, let's talk about mutual funds and exchange-traded funds (ETFs). These investment funds pool money from many investors and invest in a diversified portfolio of stocks, bonds, or other assets. They offer a convenient way to diversify investments and spread risk across different assets.

While investing has growth potential, it's essential to understand that it also carries risks. Prices in the stock market can fluctuate, and the value of investments can go up or down. That's why it's crucial to invest with a long-term mindset and avoid making emotional decisions based on short-term fluctuations. Try not to time the market; invest for the long term.

To get started with investing, you'll need a brokerage account. This is like a digital wallet where you buy and sell investments. Many brokerage platforms have user-friendly interfaces, making it easy for beginners to navigate and make informed decisions. As a person under 21 or 18 in some states, you will need to have a custodian (adult) help you set up the account. The custodian receives communication from the brokerage and acts as the point of contact for the account. Even though they have access to the account, the money is not the custodians; it is yours to buy, sell or withdraw if you like.

Lastly, remember that investing is not a get-rich-quick scheme; it's a journey that requires patience and learning. Take the time to educate yourself about different investment options, understand your risk tolerance, and set clear financial goals.

Ultimately, investing offers an exciting opportunity to grow your money and secure your financial future. By understanding the various investment options, managing risks, and staying informed, you'll be on your way to becoming a savvy investor, ready to seize the opportunities that come your way. So, embrace the power of investing and let your money work for you as you embark on this transformative financial journey.

Basic Understanding Of Investing And How It Helps Grow Money Over Time

Investing in the stock market or bond market can be an excellent way to grow your money over time.

Let's explore how each of these markets can work its magic:

Stock Market: When you invest in the stock market, you become a partial owner of companies by buying shares or stocks. As these companies grow and become more profitable, the value of your shares increases. When you sell those shares later at a higher price than you bought them, you make a profit—a concept known as capital appreciation.

Many companies also pay dividends to their shareholders. Dividends are a portion of the company's profits distributed to investors regularly. By reinvesting dividends or using them to buy more shares, you can compound your returns, making your money grow faster.

Bond Market: Investing in the bond market means you're essentially lending money to governments or corporations by buying bonds. In return, these entities pay you back the principal amount plus interest over time. Bonds are generally considered safer than stocks because they offer more predictable returns. They are often used as a way to preserve capital and generate a steady stream of income. By holding onto bonds until they mature, you receive back the original investment. If you bought them at a discount, you earn the difference between the discounted price and the maturity value—a form of capital appreciation.

Diversification: The stock and bond markets offer a vast array of investment options. By diversifying your investment portfolio—spreading your money across different companies, industries, or types of bonds—, you reduce the risk of losing everything if one investment doesn't perform well.

Diversification allows you to balance potential risks and rewards, creating a more stable and resilient investment approach.

Time is Your Ally: Investing in the stock or bond markets is a long-term game. The longer you stay invested, the more your money can benefit from the power of compound growth. Time allows your investments to ride out market fluctuations and potential downturns, allowing your money to grow steadily and significantly.

However, remember that both the stock and bond markets come with risks. Prices can fluctuate, and there's no guarantee of returns. It's essential to approach investing with a long-term mindset, research, and seek advice from financial professionals.

In conclusion, investing in the stock or bond market can be a powerful tool to grow your money over time. By harnessing the forces of capital appreciation, dividends, and compound growth, you can create a path to financial prosperity and build a solid foundation for your future. Just remember to stay patient, stay informed, and embrace the potential rewards that investing can offer.

Investment Accounts, Stocks, And Bonds In Simple Terms

As we discussed before, a custodial investment account is necessary for minors until they reach the age of majority in their state for several important reasons. As a minor, you might have the ambition to start investing early and build a solid financial future. However, legal and practical considerations make custodial accounts essential for young investors.

Legal Protection: Minors are generally not allowed to enter into binding contracts or make financial decisions independently. Custodial investment accounts provide legal protection by designating an adult custodian (usually a parent or guardian) to manage and oversee the account until the minor reaches the age of majority. This ensures that all transactions and investment decisions are made in the minor's best interest and comply with the law.

Ownership and Control: While the custodian manages the account, its assets still belong to the minor. As you grow older and gain financial responsibility, you'll eventually assume control of the account when you reach the age of majority. This gradual transition empowers you to learn about investing and money management while having an experienced custodian guide you.

Education and Financial Literacy: Custodial investment accounts offer an excellent opportunity for parents and guardians to involve minors in the world of finance. It provides a hands-on learning experience, allowing you to watch your investments grow and learn about the dynamics of the financial markets. By observing the custodian's decisions and understanding the account's performance, you can develop crucial financial literacy skills from an early age.

Tax Benefits: In some cases, custodial investment accounts offer tax advantages. Earnings generated within the account may be taxed at the minor's lower tax rate, potentially resulting in tax savings compared to holding investments in the custodian's name.

Smooth Transition to Independence: As you approach the age of majority, the custodial account will transition into your control. This process enables a smooth handover of your investments and assets, allowing you to confidently take charge of your financial future.

Overall, custodial investment accounts serve as a secure and educational vehicle for minors to begin their investment journey. They provide the necessary legal framework, financial education, and tax benefits while offering a gradual transfer of control, setting young investors on a path toward financial independence and success.

The Stock Market: Buying, selling, and owning stocks is essential to investing in the stock market. When you decide to buy stocks, you purchase partial company ownership. To do this, you'll need a brokerage account—a digital platform that allows you to trade stocks. After researching various companies and identifying one that aligns with your investment goals, you place an order through your brokerage account. There are two main types of orders: a market order, which buys the stock at the current market price, and a limit order, which specifies the maximum price you're willing to pay for the stock.

Once you own a stock, you can decide when to sell it. Selling stocks follows a similar process to buying them. You place an order through your brokerage account, choosing between a market order or a limit order. Some investors sell stocks when they believe they've reached their full potential or need to reallocate their investments. In contrast, others hold onto them for the long term, taking advantage of compound growth and weathering market fluctuations.

Owning stocks means you become a shareholder of

the company. As a shareholder, you have certain rights, such as voting on corporate matters and receiving dividends if the company pays them. As you participate in the company's growth and success, owning stocks can be empowering. However, it also carries risks, as stock prices can fluctuate due to various factors. To navigate the stock market successfully, it's essential to stay informed, have a clear investment strategy, and consider diversifying your portfolio to spread risk. Remember that investing in the stock market involves risks, and it's crucial to approach it with a long-term mindset, be patient, and seek advice from financial experts when needed.

4.3 Entrepreneurship

The power of entrepreneurship is truly remarkable, as it possesses the ability to create wealth and opportunities beyond imagination. As someone who has ventured into multiple business opportunities, I have experienced firsthand entrepreneurship's transformative potential and risk. When you start a business, you are not just creating a source of income but laying the foundation for a journey that can lead to financial freedom and prosperity. Unlike traditional employment, entrepreneurship allows you to be the architect of your destiny, with the freedom to shape your path and determine the course of your success.

One of the most captivating aspects of entrepreneurship, and why it remains my favorite, is its unique ability to buy back your time and offer a genuine life/work balance. As a business owner, you have the autonomy to set your schedule and prioritize what truly matters in your life. While the initial stages of building a business may demand significant effort and dedication, the ultimate goal is to create systems and structures that can operate with minimal intervention, freeing up your time for other pursuits and passions. Entrepreneurship grants you the priceless gift of being in control of your destiny, allowing you to strike a harmonious balance between your personal and professional aspirations, nurturing both aspects of your life to flourish.

Inspiring Entrepreneurial Thinking

Entrepreneurial thinking is a mindset that fuels innovation, creativity, and the courage to pursue one's dreams by starting a small business. The spark ignites the journey of turning an idea into reality, building something from scratch, and creating positive change in the world. Embracing entrepreneurial thinking empowers individuals to challenge the status quo, identify opportunities amid challenges, and take calculated risks to achieve their goals.

Starting a small business is like embarking on an exhilarating adventure. It begins with a vision, a passion, and a desire to make a difference. Whether opening a cozy café (lemonade stand), launching a tech startup, streaming content, or offering a unique service, the possibilities are boundless. Entrepreneurship encourages individuals to step outside their comfort zones, face uncertainties, and transform obstacles into stepping stones.

One of the most valuable lessons of starting a small business is the journey of growth and self-discovery. Aspiring entrepreneurs learn to adapt, persevere through failures, and celebrate every success, no matter how small. The process instills resilience, determination, continuous improvement, and evolution.

Entrepreneurial thinking also fosters a spirit of innovation and resourcefulness. Small businesses often operate with limited resources, encouraging entrepreneurs to find creative solutions to challenges and optimize their operations. Nurturing this mindset can lead to groundbreaking ideas and inventions that reshape industries and inspire others to follow suit. We can start and grow nearly an infinite number of businesses, from plumbing to mowing yards. Some of the more recent ways individuals buy back their time are by working in an online environment, including:

1. E-commerce Stores: Launching an online store to sell products, whether through dropshipping, creating unique items, or retailing existing goods.

2. Affiliate Marketing: Partnering with companies to promote their products or services and earning a commission for each successful sale made through your referral link.

3. Blogging and Content Creation: Starting a blog or YouTube channel to share valuable content, attracting a dedicated audience, and monetizing through ads, sponsorships, or product promotions.

4. Freelancing Services: Offering specialized skills like graphic design, writing, programming, or digital marketing as a freelancer through platforms

like Upwork or Fiverr.

5. Online Courses and E-books: Creating and selling online courses or e-books on subjects you excel in or have expertise in. Like this book, I am a financial advisor and entrepreneur writing on a topic I have years of experience in and providing that information to you.

6. App and Software Development: Developing mobile apps, software, or web applications to cater to specific needs and selling them on app stores or through licensing.

7. Virtual Coaching and Consulting: Through virtual sessions, providing coaching or consulting services in areas like life coaching, business development, or career guidance.

8. Print-on-Demand Business: Designing and selling custom merchandise like t-shirts, mugs, and phone cases without maintaining inventory through print-on-demand services.

9. Dropshipping: Partnering with suppliers to sell their products directly to customers without holding inventory and handling order fulfillment.

10. Online Gaming and Streaming: Becoming a video game streamer on platforms like Twitch or YouTube, entertaining an audience while earning

revenue through ads, donations, or sponsorships.

These entrepreneurial ideas showcase the vast opportunities available in the online realm, catering to various interests, skills, and passions. From creating engaging content to selling products and services, the digital landscape offers an array of paths to turn creativity and ambition into lucrative online ventures.

Furthermore, small businesses are vital in driving economic growth and job creation. They inject dynamism into local communities, contributing to a vibrant and diverse business landscape. Entrepreneurs become change-makers, not only in their own lives but also in the lives of those they employ and the customers they serve.

However, the path of entrepreneurship is not without its challenges. It requires dedication, sacrifice, and a willingness to learn from setbacks. Yet, the rewards can be immeasurable. The satisfaction of seeing a dream come to life, the impact on customers and communities, and the potential for financial success are all compelling reasons to embrace the small business world.

Finally, inspiring entrepreneurial thinking is essential in today's ever-changing world. By encouraging individuals to start small businesses, we foster a culture of innovation, independence, and resilience. Through entrepreneurship, individuals can unleash their full potential, create value, and leave a lasting legacy. Aspiring entrepreneurs should be encouraged to take that leap of faith, armed with a passion for their vision and a determination to make a difference. The journey may be challenging, but the rewards can be extraordinary, making the world better, one small business at a time.

Encouraging Creativity, Problem-Solving, And Financial Independence

As you embark on this exciting journey, I encourage you to embrace your creativity, problem-solving skills, and financial independence wholeheartedly. These traits will be your secret weapons, propelling you toward success and helping you take charge of your life, time, and cash flow.

Creativity is your superpower! Don't be afraid to think outside the box, dream big, and explore new ideas. Whether starting a business or creating content online, your unique perspective and innovative thinking will set you apart. Be curious, ask questions, and be open to inspiration from unexpected sources. Remember, your creativity will make your ventures stand out and resonate with your audience.

You'll face challenges along the way, but don't let them deter you. Embrace problem-solving like a fearless adventurer!
Approach obstacles as opportunities to grow and learn.
Analyze the issues, seek advice, and come up with clever
solutions. Your ability to overcome hurdles will build resilience and confidence, paving the way for even greater achievements.

As you dive into your entrepreneurial journey, remember the importance of financial independence. Manage your money wisely and take control of your finances early on. Always keep your business and your personal budgets separate. Budgeting and saving will give you the freedom to pursue your dreams without unnecessary stress. Learn about investments and how to grow your money smartly. Financial independence will grant you the power to make choices aligned with your values and aspirations.

So, young entrepreneur, let your creativity soar, embrace problem-solving fearlessly, and seize financial independence. This journey will be a rollercoaster ride, but with your determination and these essential traits, you'll be well-equipped to take control of your destiny. Remember, the path to success might not be smooth, but with each step, you'll grow, learn, and build your dream life.

Believe in yourself, trust your instincts, and let your entrepreneurial spirit guide you toward greatness. The world awaits your ideas and creations, so go out there and make your mark!

4.4 Building a Rainy-Day Fund

I cannot over-emphasize the importance of building a rainy-day fund - a safety net that can save the day when unexpected financial storms hit. Life is full of surprises, and having some cash stashed away for emergencies can be a game-changer.

Imagine this: you're enjoying life, and suddenly your phone stops working, or your laptop decides to call it quits. Or maybe your car needs unexpected repairs, and you have a job interview the next day. That's where your rainy-day fund comes to the rescue! Having money set aside for these unexpected moments means you won't have to stress about handling these situations or resort to borrowing money.

Building a rainy-day fund is about taking control of your financial future. It gives you the freedom to handle challenges without derailing your long-term plans. Plus, having this cushion of cash can ease your mind and reduce stress when unexpected things happen. It's like having a superhero cape ready to save the day!

Start small, save consistently, and watch your rainy-day fund grow. Even setting aside a little money each week can add up to a significant amount when you need it most. So, let's take charge of our financial well-being and start building that rainy-day fund today. Your future self will thank you when those rainy days become opportunities for strength and resilience!

Building An Emergency Fund For Unexpected Expenses

I had a client named Sarah, a hardworking young adult just starting her career. She had recently started saving money in a rainy-day fund, inspired by the advice of her financial advisor. At first, Sarah wasn't entirely convinced of the importance of this fund, but she decided to try it and set aside a portion of her monthly income.

One day, as Sarah was driving to work, her car suddenly broke down on a busy highway. Panicked and unsure of what to do, she remembered her rainy-day fund. With a sense of relief, she called for a tow truck and covered the repair expenses from her savings. Sarah would have been stranded without that safety net, struggling to pay for the unexpected repairs.

Not long after, another unexpected event occurred. Sarah's apartment building suffered a severe water leak, causing significant damage to her belongings and disrupting her living situation. With her rainy-day fund already in place, Sarah could cover temporary accommodation expenses and replace damaged items without any financial strain.

As the months passed, Sarah diligently contributed to her rainy-day fund. Little did she know that her wise decision would have a more significant impact in the future. One day, her dream job opportunity arose in a different city, and she couldn't pass it up. Moving to a new place was costly, but thanks to her well-funded rainy-day account, Sarah had the means to cover moving expenses, secure a new place, and transition smoothly to her new job.

With each life twist and turn, Sarah's rainy-day fund provided the security she needed to navigate challenges without derailing her financial goals. The fund became her reliable ally, empowering her to take control of her life and enjoy peace of mind amidst the unpredictability of life's ups and downs.

Sarah's story is a testament to the transformative power of a rainy-day fund. Having that financial safety net allowed her to weather the storms of unexpected events and seize opportunities that came her way. It was a reminder that no matter what life throws her way, Sarah's wise decision to save for a rainy day made all the difference in securing her financial well-being and creating a brighter future.

Three Techniques To Save Money For Unforeseen Situations

1. Create a Dedicated Emergency Fund: A crucial strategy is to establish a separate savings account specifically for emergencies. Set a monthly savings goal and prioritize contributions to this fund. Aim to save three to six months' worth of living expenses to provide a solid financial cushion in unexpected occurrences like job loss, medical emergencies, or urgent repairs.

2. Automate Savings: Utilize automation to make saving a seamless process. Set up automatic transfers from your checking account to your emergency fund or other savings accounts. By automating savings, you remove the temptation to spend the money elsewhere, consistently making it easier to build your savings over time.

3. Cut Discretionary Spending: Take a close look at your spending habits and identify areas where you can cut back. Forgo unnecessary expenses like eating out frequently, impulsive purchases, or excessive online subscriptions. Redirect the money

you save from these cutbacks into your emergency fund. By consciously managing your spending, you'll free up funds to build your financial safety net.

Implementing these three techniques can help you save money effectively for unexpected occurrences. Remember that building a strong financial foundation takes time and discipline, but the security and peace of mind it provides during challenging times are well worth the effort.

4.5 Financial Responsibility and Philanthropy

"Financial responsibility is the foundation upon which we build our lives, embracing virtue in both abundance and scarcity. In cultivating mindful stewardship of our resources, we gain mastery over desires, fostering resilience amidst life's uncertainties. Yet, let not the pursuit of wealth obscure the higher purpose of our existence. Philanthropy, the noble art of giving, imparts true richness to our souls, for in the act of benevolence, we find communion with humanity's collective journey. Embrace the balance of prudence and compassion, and in the embrace of financial responsibility and philanthropy, discover the profound harmony of a life well-lived."

Values Of Financial Responsibility And Giving Back To Society

1. Integrity: Upholding honesty and transparency in financial dealings, fostering trust and credibility in personal and societal interactions.

2. Accountability: Taking ownership of financial decisions, learning from mistakes, and striving for continuous improvement.

3. Self-Discipline: Exercising restraint in spending, saving consistently, and adhering to a financial plan.

4. Long-Term Vision: Planning for the future, setting financial goals, and making choices that align with broader aspirations.

5. Generosity: Giving back to society through charitable donations, volunteering time, and supporting meaningful causes.

6. Gratitude: Recognizing the blessings of abundance and expressing appreciation for the opportunities to help others.

7. Community Engagement: Engaging with local communities, supporting local businesses, and actively participating in initiatives that promote positive change.

8. Environmental Consciousness: Integrating sustainable practices into financial decisions, considering the impact on the environment and future generations.

9. Empathy: Understanding the struggles of others and extending compassion to those in need, fostering a sense of shared responsibility.

10. Social Impact: Evaluating financial decisions

based not only on personal gain but also on their potential to contribute positively to society.

By embracing these values of financial responsibility and giving back to society, individuals can cultivate a sense of purpose and fulfillment in their financial journey, leaving a lasting impact on their lives and the lives of others.

Exploring Opportunities For Philanthropy And Making A Positive Impact

There are numerous opportunities for individuals to get involved in philanthropic giving and positively impact their communities and beyond. One option is to support local charitable organizations or nonprofits that align with personal values and causes. Whether contributing to a food bank, an animal shelter, or an educational program, donating to these organizations can help address pressing needs and uplift those facing challenges.

Another opportunity is to participate in community initiatives and volunteer activities. Giving back one's time and skills can be equally impactful as financial donations. Engaging in local events, clean-up drives, or mentorship programs allows individuals to directly contribute to community growth and create meaningful connections with others.

Lastly, consider launching personal philanthropic projects or campaigns. Utilize social media platforms or crowdfunding websites to raise awareness and funds for specific causes. Initiating a charitable project can empower individuals to drive change on their terms and mobilize others to join the cause.

Philanthropic giving offers a fulfilling pathway to make a difference in the lives of others. By exploring these opportunities, individuals can contribute to the betterment of society, cultivate a sense of purpose, and inspire others to do the same. Remember, even small giving can create a ripple effect, making the world a better place one compassionate gesture at a time.

CHAPTER 5
MAKING SMART
FINANCIAL
CHOICES

"Embrace the wisdom of discernment in your financial choices, for in prudent deliberation lies the key to prosperous and purposeful living."

5.1 Consumer Awareness

There is power in consumer awareness and making smart financial choices. It's an essential skill that will serve you well throughout life. Consumer awareness means being mindful of your choices when spending your hard-earned money. Before making a purchase, take a moment to consider if it aligns with your needs and values. Don't be swayed by flashy advertisements or peer pressure. Instead, focus on what truly brings value and happiness to your life.

One of the keys to smart financial choices is understanding the concept of "value for money." It's not just about finding the cheapest option; it's about getting the most out of your spending. Compare prices, read reviews, and consider the quality and durability of products. Remember, the best choice isn't always the most expensive one either. Sometimes, a lower-priced item can offer the same value or even more!

Another aspect of consumer awareness is avoiding impulse purchases. We all get those sudden urges to buy something but try to take a step back and think it through. Ask yourself if it's something you truly need or if it's just a passing desire. Give yourself time to reflect before making a decision. By doing so, you'll avoid regretful purchases and have more resources available for things that truly matter in the long run. In the end, practicing consumer awareness and making smart financial choices will empower you to take control of your money and lead a more intentional and fulfilling life.

Encouraging Critical Thinking Skills When It Comes To Advertising And Marketing

In a world inundated with advertising and marketing messages, developing critical thinking skills is paramount. Remember, marketers' primary goal is to convince you to purchase their products, and they may not always act ethically. When encountering advertisements, be vigilant and question the claims they make. Ask yourself: Does this product genuinely solve a problem I have? Is it as amazing as they claim it to be? Is there evidence to support their promises?

Learn to distinguish between emotional appeals and rational decision-making. Marketers often use emotions to trigger impulsive purchases, but a thoughtful approach involves evaluating the true value of a product or service. Look beyond flashy slogans and captivating visuals; instead, seek out honest reviews and opinions from trusted sources.

Be mindful of manipulative tactics, such as scarcity marketing or fear-based messaging. The urgency to buy can sometimes be an artificial construct to pressure you into making hasty decisions. Think of a limited-time offer, or buy today while supplies last. Take your time, do your research, and trust your instincts. A well-informed consumer is a powerful one, able to make choices that align with their needs and values.

In cultivating critical thinking skills, you become more than just a passive recipient of advertising. You become empowered, capable of seeing through deceptive practices and making sound decisions based on facts and thoughtful consideration. By questioning marketing messages and staying true to your principles, you safeguard yourself against impulsive purchases and pave the way for a more mindful and financially responsible future.

Make Informed Decisions And Avoid Unnecessary Purchases

I had the pleasure of working with a client named Bill, a young professional eager to achieve financial freedom. Bill had always been enthusiastic about the latest gadgets and tech trends, often making impulse purchases without considering their value. As we delved into his financial habits, it became apparent that this impulsive spending hindered his ability to save for more important goals.

Together, we embarked on a financial education journey, focusing on making informed decisions and avoiding unnecessary purchases. We discussed the importance of distinguishing between wants and needs and how a well-thought-out purchase could align with his long-term aspirations. Slowly, Bill began to cultivate a more thoughtful approach to spending.

One day, as we reviewed his budget, Bill excitedly shared news about the latest smartphone hitting the market. He would have rushed to pre-order it in the past, but this time, he hesitated. Applying the critical thinking skills he had learned, he researched the phone's features, read reviews, and considered how it would truly benefit his life.

After much consideration, Bill decided to hold off on the purchase. Instead, he diverted the funds into his savings, setting his sights on a future trip he had always dreamed of. It was a transformative moment for Bill as he realized that by making informed decisions, he could prioritize experiences and goals that brought greater fulfillment and lasting happiness.

As our journey together continued, Bill's newfound discipline in avoiding unnecessary purchases started to pay off. He saw his savings grow, and the sense of financial control empowered him to pursue bigger dreams. In time, Bill achieved his dream of traveling abroad, exploring new cultures, and immersing himself in unforgettable experiences—all thanks to the wisdom of making thoughtful and informed choices.

Through this experience, Bill learned that true wealth lies not in accumulating material possessions but in making choices that align with one's values and aspirations. Making informed decisions became his guiding principle, leading him on a path of financial freedom and a life filled with purpose and meaningful accomplishments.

5.2 Credit and Debt

L et's get into credit and debt - a crucial aspect of personal finance you'll encounter as you grow into adulthood. Credit is like a financial tool that allows you to borrow money from banks or lenders for various purposes, such as buying a car, going to college, or even purchasing a home. It's important to understand that credit can be beneficial when used responsibly, but it can also lead to financial challenges if not managed wisely.

When you borrow money from a lender, you create a debt you need to repay over time, often with interest. Interest is essentially the cost of borrowing money, and paying attention to the interest rates and terms of your loans is essential. Taking on debt should be a well-considered decision, as it affects your financial health in the long run. Suppose you use credit responsibly and make timely payments. In that case, it can help you build a positive credit history, which is essential for future financial endeavors, such as renting an apartment or getting a loan for a business.

However, understanding your financial limits is the

key to responsibly handling credit and debt. It's easy to get carried away and accumulate excessive debt, leading to overwhelming financial stress. As you start using credit, make sure to create a budget and track your spending to ensure you can comfortably repay any debts you take on. Avoid maxing out credit cards or taking on more loans than you can handle, as this can lead to a debt spiral that's challenging to escape.

In summary, credit and debt can be valuable tools but require responsible management. Educate yourself about the terms, interest rates, and potential consequences of borrowing money. By making informed decisions and using credit wisely, you'll be better equipped to navigate the world of personal finance, building a strong foundation for a successful and secure financial future. Remember, knowledge is power, and arming yourself with financial literacy is one of the most valuable skills you can develop as you embark on your journey to adulthood.

Introducing The Concepts Of Credit, Loans, And Debt

Credit, loans, and debt - essential concepts that play a significant role in personal finance. Let's start with credit. Think of credit as a financial trust that lenders, like banks or credit card companies, place in you to repay borrowed money. When you use a credit card or take out a loan, you borrow money to make purchases or cover expenses. This allows you to buy things you need or want without paying for them all at once. However, remember that credit is not free money; it's a loan you must repay, usually with interest.

Now, loans are one of the primary ways individuals borrow money. When you take out a loan, you agree to repay the money over time, often with interest. There are various types of loans, such as student loans for education, car loans for purchasing a vehicle, and mortgage loans for buying a home. Loans can help you achieve significant goals and invest in your future, but they also come with responsibilities. Reading and understanding the loan terms, including interest rates, repayment schedules, and any fees involved, is essential.

Debt is a result of borrowing money through credit or loans. When you use credit or take on a loan, you create a debt you must repay. Managing debt is a crucial part of your financial journey. While some debt can be beneficial like student loans that enable you to get an education, accumulating too much debt without a plan to repay it can lead to financial stress. Being responsible for debt means borrowing only what you can afford to pay back and making regular and timely payments. Building a good credit history by handling debt responsibly is vital, as it impacts your ability to borrow money in the future and may affect other aspects of your financial life, such as renting an apartment or getting insurance.

You must practice good financial habits as you navigate the world of credit, loans, and debt. Always spend within your means, and avoid borrowing more than you can comfortably repay. Creating a budget will help you track your spending and meet your financial obligations. Remember, using credit and loans responsibly can open doors to various opportunities and financial growth. Still, it's essential to be informed, make thoughtful decisions, and prioritize your long-term financial well-being. Building a strong foundation of financial literacy now will empower you to make informed choices, achieve your goals, and set yourself up for a successful and secure future.

Discussing Responsible Credit Card Usage And The Potential Risks Of Excessive Debt

Let's have a candid chat about responsible credit card usage and the potential risks. Credit cards can be handy financial tools, providing convenience and flexibility when purchasing. However, they also come with significant responsibilities that you must be aware of to avoid falling into a debt trap.

Responsible credit card usage means using your card

wisely and within your means. It's crucial only to charge what you can afford to pay back in full each month to avoid accumulating high-interest debt. Make sure to keep track of your spending and stick to a budget to ensure you don't overspend. Paying your credit card bill on time and in full demonstrates financial responsibility and helps build a positive credit history, which is crucial for future financial endeavors.

Conversely, excessive credit card debt can lead to financial troubles. High-interest rates on unpaid balances can quickly escalate, making it challenging to pay off the debt. This can lead to a cycle of minimum payments, where you end up paying much more in interest than the actual purchases you made. Additionally, excessive debt can negatively impact your credit score, affecting your ability to get loans, rent an apartment, or secure favorable insurance rates.

To safeguard yourself from potential risks, treat your credit card as a tool, not a source of free money. If you're unsure about making a purchase, take a moment to consider if it's a necessity or a want. Remember, being mindful of your credit card usage and practicing responsible financial habits will lead you toward a more secure and prosperous future. Educate yourself about the terms and conditions of your credit card, and use it to build a positive credit history and gain valuable financial experience. By making informed decisions and handling credit responsibly, you'll be better equipped to navigate the world of personal finance and achieve your financial goals.

5.3 Identity Theft and Online Security

I had a client named Michael who experienced a devastating encounter with identity theft and online security breaches. It all began when he received a suspicious email that appeared to be from his bank, asking him to verify his account details urgently. Innocently, he clicked on the link and entered his personal information, not suspecting it was a cleverly disguised phishing scam.

Before long, Michael started noticing unusual transactions on his bank statements and received notifications of new credit accounts opened in his name. He was horrified to realize that he had fallen victim to identity theft. The repercussions were significant, with substantial financial losses and a prolonged period of stress and frustration as he worked to resolve the issue.

Michael committed to developing good online security habits to protect himself from future cyber threats. He became diligent about changing his passwords regularly, using solid and unique combinations for each account. He also started using two-factor authentication whenever possible to add an extra layer of protection. Additionally, he invested in reputable anti-virus software to safeguard his devices from malware and potential hacking attempts.

As time passed, Michael's dedication to online security paid off. Knowing he had fortified his digital defenses, he no longer feared identity theft. He also took the time to educate his family and friends about the importance of online safety, sharing his story as a cautionary tale to protect others from falling prey to cyber threats.

Michael's journey reminds us that our digital lives require as much protection and care as our physical well-being. By adopting good habits and remaining vigilant, we can shield ourselves from online vulnerabilities and safeguard our hard-earned money and personal information. Michael's newfound dedication to online security ultimately became an empowering shield that kept him safe from harm and enabled him to navigate the digital landscape with confidence and peace of mind.

Educating Children About The Importance Of Protecting Personal And Financial Information

So, it is critically important to safeguard your

personal and financial information. In today's digital age, protecting your data is like building a fortress to keep your castle safe. Your personal information, like your name, address, and social media details, is valuable and should be treated carefully.

Always be cautious about sharing sensitive information online or with strangers. Use privacy settings on social media platforms to control who can see your posts and information. Be careful about the links you click on and emails you open, as cybercriminals often try to trick you into revealing your data.

When it comes to financial information, like your bank account details or credit card numbers, keep it under lock and key. Never share these details unless you are sure of the request's legitimacy. Create strong and unique passwords for your accounts, and consider using two-factor authentication for added security. You can build a solid defense against identity theft and online scams by being vigilant and informed. Protecting your personal and financial information is not just about keeping your castle secure; it's about maintaining control over your life and peace of mind in this digital world. Stay smart and stay safe!

Discussing Online Safety And Strategies

To Prevent Identity Theft

Online security is crucial in today's digital world. Here are the top three ways to protect yourself and avoid identity theft:

Strong Passwords: Create unique and strong passwords for all your accounts using a combination of letters, numbers, and symbols.
Avoid using easily guessable information like your name or birthdate. Consider using a password manager to keep track of your passwords securely.

Two-Factor Authentication (2FA): Enable 2FA wherever possible. This adds an extra layer of security by requiring a second verification, such as a code sent to your phone and your password.

Beware of Scams: Be cautious of emails or messages from unknown sources, especially if they ask for personal information or prompt you to click on suspicious links. Never share sensitive data with anyone you don't trust.

By following these strategies, you can significantly reduce the risk of falling victim to identity theft and stay safe while enjoying the benefits of the online world. Stay vigilant and keep your castle secure!

5.4 Financial Success and Happiness

While money can play a role in achieving specific goals and providing comfort, true happiness goes beyond material possessions. Financial success is not solely measured by the size of your bank account but by how well you manage your money and live within your means. Money isn't everything, but as the country music star stated, "It can buy me a boat."

Setting realistic financial goals and developing good money habits early on is essential. Save a portion of your future earnings, whether for college, a dream vacation, or starting a business. Prioritize needs over wants and avoid falling into the trap of impulsive spending. Budgeting is your secret weapon, helping you allocate your money wisely and plan for a secure future.

Remember that true happiness comes from finding joy in experiences, relationships, and personal growth. Nurture meaningful connections with family and friends, and invest time pursuing your passions and hobbies. Practice gratitude for what you have, focusing on what truly matters.

While financial success can open doors and provide opportunities, it's not the sole factor in leading a fulfilling life. Strive for a balance between financial responsibility and personal fulfillment. Pursue a career or vocation that aligns with your interests and values, where you can make a positive impact. Finally, financial success is a part of life, but viewing it from perspective is essential. Manage your finances wisely and cherish experiences and relationships that bring joy and meaning to your life. By finding the right balance and embracing financial responsibility and personal fulfillment, you'll be on the path to a truly happy and successful life.

Reinforcing The Idea That Economic Success Goes Beyond Material Possessions

In life's journey, financial success goes beyond the accumulation of material possessions. While having financial stability can provide comfort and opportunities, true wealth lies in the richness of experiences, relationships, and personal growth. It's about finding fulfillment in the moments that money can't buy. As we talked about before, buying back your time through strict work-life balance, entrepreneurship, and remembering that if you didn't go to work tomorrow, that company would find a replacement within a few days.

Instead of chasing the latest gadgets or trendiest fashion, focus on investing in yourself and your dreams. Cultivate a growth mindset, embrace learning, and discover your passions. Pursuing meaningful goals and nurturing your talents can lead to a sense of purpose and satisfaction that lasts a lifetime.

Value the time spent with loved ones, building memories, and supporting each other through thick and thin. Happiness is often found in shared laughter, heartfelt conversations, and the comfort of being surrounded by those who care for you.

Remember that financial success should not define your self-worth. Instead of comparing yourself to others' possessions or social media appearances, appreciate the unique journey that you're on. Embrace gratitude for what you have, and let contentment be your compass in this ever-changing world.

In the end, financial success is a tool that can provide opportunities, but it is not the ultimate measure of a fulfilled life. Seek balance in your aspirations and values, and remember that true wealth comes from fostering a sense of joy, purpose, and genuine connection with yourself and the world around you.

Emphasizing The Importance Of Personal Values, Relationships, And Happiness In Relation To Money

In money and personal finance, it's crucial to emphasize the profound connection between our values, relationships, and happiness. While cash can offer comfort and security, its true worth lies in how it aligns with our innermost values and the joy it brings to our lives and the lives of others.

Understanding our values is the cornerstone of making sound financial decisions. By identifying what truly matters to us, we can allocate our resources in meaningful and fulfilling ways. Our values guide us in setting financial goals that resonate with our beliefs, whether supporting causes we are passionate about or prioritizing experiences with loved ones over material possessions.

Moreover, the quality of our relationships dramatically influences our happiness and overall well-being. Healthy connections with family, friends, and community build a robust support system beyond monetary boundaries. True wealth emerges when we cultivate genuine relationships based on trust, empathy, and compassion.

Rather than viewing money as an end in itself, it's essential to recognize it as a tool to enhance our happiness and the happiness of others. Financial decisions should consider the potential impact on our well-being and those around us. Practicing mindful spending, giving back to the community, and engaging in philanthropy can bring immense satisfaction and purpose to our lives.

Real happiness and fulfillment arise from a harmonious balance between financial choices, values, and relationships. By aligning our money decisions with our true desires and investing in what truly matters, we unlock the potential for genuine happiness and a life rich in the truest sense. Emphasizing the significance of personal values, meaningful relationships, and lasting happiness in relation to money can lead us on a path of true abundance and contentment.

REVIEW AND RECAP

Responsibly managing money is a fundamental skill that lays the foundation for a secure and prosperous future. Throughout this financial journey, we have explored various key aspects of financial literacy, each serving as a stepping stone toward financial empowerment.

Setting clear and achievable goals is the first step toward financial success. Defining our short-term and long-term objectives gives us direction and motivation to stay focused on our financial journey. Whether saving for college, starting a business, or building an emergency fund, goal-setting empowers us to make informed financial decisions that align with our aspirations.

Budgeting is an essential tool for managing money effectively. By creating a budget, we gain insight into our income, expenses, and savings, allowing us to prioritize needs over wants and curb impulsive spending. Budgeting also aids in building a safety net, preparing us for unforeseen circumstances and allowing us to handle financial challenges confidently.

The world of entrepreneurship opens doors to financial independence and the freedom to pursue our passions. By embracing entrepreneurial thinking, we cultivate creativity and problem-solving skills, which are vital in today's dynamic business landscape. Entrepreneurship enables us to control our time and cash flow, creating personal and financial growth opportunities.

Work-life balance is equally crucial as we navigate the path to financial success. While striving for professional accomplishments, we must remember to cherish moments with loved ones and prioritize our well-being. Balancing work and personal life contributes to happiness and enhances our ability to make sound financial decisions.

Identity theft and online safety are constant challenges in the digital age. We must remain vigilant and adopt smart practices to safeguard ourselves from cyber threats. Regularly changing passwords, using two-factor authentication, and being cautious of phishing scams are essential to protecting our personal and financial information.

In conclusion, the journey toward financial

literacy has been enlightening and empowering. By managing money responsibly, setting clear goals, budgeting wisely, and exploring the world of entrepreneurship, we have gained valuable tools to take charge of our financial destinies. Balancing work and personal life has allowed us to enjoy professional accomplishments and cherished relationships. Additionally, we can safeguard our digital lives and maintain our financial security by understanding the importance of identity theft prevention and online safety.

As we continue our financial learning journey, let us keep these valuable lessons close to heart. By being mindful of our financial choices and nurturing our financial well-being, we pave the way for a prosperous future. May we embrace financial literacy as a lifelong pursuit, empowering ourselves and our communities to thrive in endless opportunities and possibilities?

The Journey Begins

Congratulations on completing this financial learning journey! As you close this book, remember that your financial education doesn't end here. Instead, view it as a stepping stone towards a lifelong financial literacy and empowerment journey. The knowledge and skills you've acquired are invaluable tools that will serve you well in all aspects of life.

Continue exploring and seeking new learning opportunities about money management, budgeting, saving, and investing. Stay curious and open-minded, as the world of finance is ever-evolving. Look for online courses, workshops, or seminars that delve deeper into financial topics that interest you. Engage with financial experts and seek advice from mentors who can guide you.

Remember, the best way to learn is through practice and experience. Take charge of your finances, and be proactive in making smart financial decisions. Whether managing an allowance, saving for a goal, or even starting a small business, each financial experience will provide valuable lessons.

Additionally, stay informed about current economic trends and financial news. Understanding the bigger picture can help you make informed decisions in an interconnected global economy. Follow reputable financial publications and watch educational videos to stay updated.

Lastly, share your knowledge and experiences with others. By teaching your friends and family about financial literacy, you'll reinforce your understanding and create a ripple effect of financial empowerment in your community.

In the end, remember that financial learning is a continuous journey of growth and empowerment. Embrace the opportunities that come your way, stay curious, and keep building on your financial knowledge. Taking charge of your financial future unlocks the potential for a lifetime of financial freedom and success. Keep learning, keep growing, and remember that the power to shape your financial destiny lies in your hands. You've got this!

ABOUT THE AUTHOR
Joshua Paulus

Meet Joshua Paulus, a seasoned and dedicated financial advisor on a mission to champion financial literacy for all, especially the young generation. With an unwavering commitment to closing the knowledge and information gap between the  financial industry and individuals, Joshua is on a quest to ensure everyone can navigate the financial landscape confidently and securely. Through his expertise and passion, he strives to minimize the potential for fraud and mismanagement of hard-earned money, empowering individuals to make informed financial decisions.

Beyond his professional pursuits, Joshua finds fulfillment as a devoted husband to his wife, Kristen, with whom he has shared two decades. Together, they have raised two wonderful adult children, Gabriel and Lukas, instilling in them the values of responsibility and financial savvy from an early age.

When he's not busy advising clients and empowering individuals with financial wisdom, Joshua dedicates his spare time to coaching youth and adult lacrosse teams. His commitment to mentoring and guiding young athletes goes hand-in-hand with his passion for educating and empowering the next generation financially.

Joshua's academic achievements further underpin his dedication to his field. He earned his Bachelor of Science in Business Administration (BSBA) from Old Dominion University, specializing in finance, laying the foundation for a successful career in the financial industry. Subsequently, he pursued an MBA from the City University of Seattle, honing his skills as a well-rounded professional.

Ever the avid learner, Joshua is currently in the final stages of completing his doctoral dissertation, focusing on Conflict of Interest in Financial Advice and its Impact on the Professionalization of the Industry. His research aims to shed light on critical aspects of the financial advisory world, driving improvements and fostering a higher standard of service.

In Joshua Paulus, you will find a dedicated financial advisor, educator, and coach driven by a profound sense of purpose. Through his tireless efforts in promoting financial literacy, he aspires to empower individuals with the knowledge and tools needed to navigate the economic realm confidently, fostering a world where financial security and prosperity are within reach for all.